Love Magic

Love Magic

A HANDBOOK OF SPELLS, CHARMS, AND POTIONS

ANASTASIA GREYWOLF

WITH ORIGINAL ILLUSTRATIONS

BY MELISSA WEST

WELLFLEET
PRESS

Brimming with creative inspiration, how-to projects, and useful information to enrich your everyday life, Quarto Knows is a favorite destination for those pursuing their interests and passions. Visit our site and dig deeper with our books into your area of interest: Quarto Creates, Quarto Cooks, Quarto Homes, Quarto Lives, Quarto Drives, Quarto Explores, Quarto Gifts, or Quarto Kids.

Text © 2018 Green Tiger and Associates
llustrations © Melissa West

First published in 2018 by Wellfleet Press,
an imprint of The Quarto Group,
142 West 36th Street, 4th Floor
New York, New York 10018
T (212) 779-4972 **F** (212) 779-6058
www.QuartoKnows.com

All rights reserved. No part of this book may be reproduced in any form without written permission of the copyright owners. All images in this book have been reproduced with the knowledge and prior consent of the artists concerned, and no responsibility is accepted by producer, publisher, or printer for any infringement of copyright or otherwise, arising from the contents of this publication. Every effort has been made to ensure that credits accurately comply with information supplied. We apologize for any inaccuracies that may have occurred and will resolve inaccurate or missing information in a subsequent reprinting of the book.

10 9 8 7 6 5 4 3

ISBN: 978-1-57715-166-1

A Green Tiger Book
Cover and Interior Design: Susan Livingston
Cover Illustrations from Shutterstock; Bottle by Kite-Kit;
Frame by AccantStudio

Printed in China

For entertainment purposes only. Do not attempt any spell, recipe, procedure, or prescription in this book. The author, publisher, packager, manufacturer, distributor, and their collective agents waive all liability for the reader's use or application of any of the text herein.

―――――∙∙◂◦∞◦▸∙∙―――――

I conjure thee, O book, to be useful unto all who fall under love's spell and who shall have recourse to use thee to settle their affairs. I conjure thee anew, to be service unto all those who shall read thee. I commit love to fill thy pages whether open or closed.

―――――∙∙◂◦∞◦▸∙∙―――――

CONTENTS

INTRODUCTION + 1
    WHAT IS LOVE MAGIC? + 2
    HOW TO PERFORM LOVE MAGIC + 4
    CASTING A CIRCLE + 5
    WRITING YOUR OWN SPELLS + 6
    THE TOOLS OF LOVE MAGIC + 7

PLATONIC LOVE AND ANIMAL FRIENDS + 11

DATING AND FINDING LOVE + 53

SPELLS TO SEE YOUR
LOVE LIFE'S FUTURE + 91

PASSION AND ROMANCE SPELLS + 111

SPELLS TO DISPEL TROUBLE
AND MAKE LOVE LAST + 131

SPELLS AND BLESSINGS FOR
MARRIAGE AND ENGAGEMENTS + 165

SPELLS AND POTIONS TO END
A LOVE OR RELATIONSHIP + 185

LISTS OF SYMBOLS AND OMENS + 211
    LOVE OMENS + 212
    LOVE BIRDS + 222
    MOON PHASES AND LOVE MAGIC + 225
    LUCKY DAYS FOR LOVE + 226
    LOVE STONES + 227
    LOVE COLORS + 230
    LOVE FLOWERS + 231
    LOVE HERBS AND SPICES + 234
    ESSENTIAL OILS USED IN LOVE MAGIC + 237

CONTRIBUTORS + 239

INDEX + 243

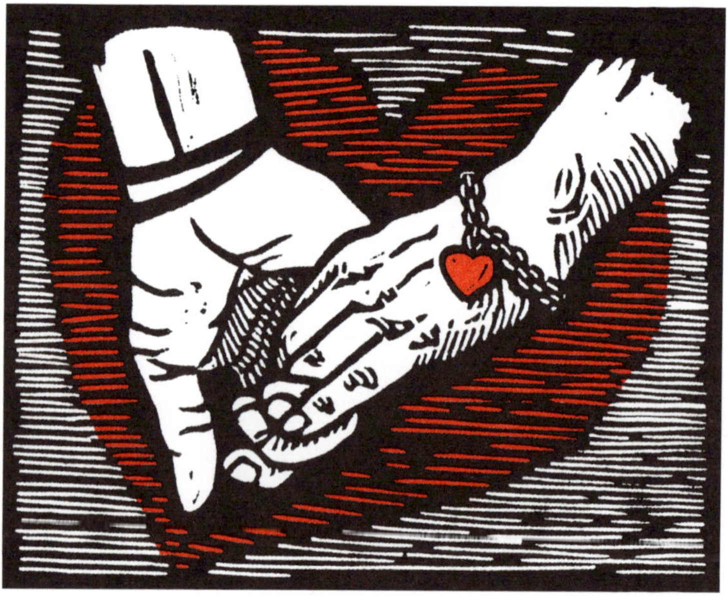

INTRODUCTION

What Is Love Magic?

Of all the mysterious forces in the universe, love may be the most powerful. For, at the end and beginning of each day, it is often those we love we think of. Having love in your life—whether in the form of a significant other, good friend, pet, relative, or even a brand new acquaintance who you've bonded with—can make even the worst days possible. However, love is hard to control, and anyone who's experienced love has also experienced negative emotions related to it as well. We thirst for it like water, yet it can cause us pain as acute as physically being broken open.

The mystic, magic nature of love makes our world go round. Weddings, the ultimate celebrations of love, are often the most memorable, magical days of our lives, whether it's our own wedding or that of a loved one. Falling in love is one of the most powerful feelings you can experience, and can leave you feeling like you're floating on air. Conversely, losing love can be one the hardest times we can endure, but it can also cause monumental shifts for good. Moments of transition between finding love can be the ones where you grow more than any

INTRODUCTION

other. And then, you find yourself thinking of love again, wondering how to find it, imagining it's found you, and waiting impatiently for your next sweetheart to walk through the door (or slide onto your screen).

In this book of love magic, I've compiled the best potions, spells, charms, and other forms of magic that can help you with all these aspects of love. Love spells have been around as long as the printed word (probably longer), and some traditional spells are included. However, most of the spells in this tome contain modern ingredients and incantations, so you can do them relatively easily with minimal ingredients. (See the following pages for some items you'll want to obtain and/or make.) Whether you want to find "the one" or simply make your pets love each other, get rid of a bad date or set yourself free from a bad energy of a relationship from the past, you'll find the magic to make it happen in these pages (check the back for a full index of spells). From more than a dozen contributors, they draw from a variety of traditions and spiritualities. I hope they help enrich the love relationships in your life.

—*Anastasia Greywolf*

How to Perform Love Magic

If you've never performed a spell or charm, it seem intimidating at first. But it's actually more straightforward than you might think—certainly more straightforward than the usual workings of love.

The efficacy of a spell depends on both your inner state of mind and what's around you. Starting from the outward looking in, prepare a space that is clean, quiet, and free of associations—unless they're associations that have to do with the spell you're about to cast. If you can't find a location that's completely free of associations, try clearing as many associations as possible out of the way in an otherwise comfortable space. For instance, to perform a spell in your bedroom, put personal items in drawers (or drape a cloth over them), and maybe even push some furniture back to clear a new space that you can start a fresh association with.

To clear the space of any past energy, especially negative energy, you can perform what's called a smudging. Light a candle and think positive thoughts. Then light some sage incense or a smudge stick (page 7) with that candle, and waft the smoke slowly around the space in a clockwise direction, remaining as calm as possible the entire time. If you're smudging an entire room, give extra attention to the corners, closet, and anywhere else negative energy or spirits could accumulate. Also spend extra

INTRODUCTION

time at the doorway. Add lavender or other herbs to it (see page 234 for herbs that have special meaning) and continue to burn while you perform your spell.

Some of the spells in this book have certain days of the week, seasons, or moon phases you should perform them on, in, or under. Others you can simply perform when you need them the most. Adapt a spell to your needs. You can leave parts out if they don't resonate with you. What's most important is to say the spell with utmost feeling and concentration. If you don't believe it, you can't except the forces in the world around you to do your bidding. So have confidence in yourself and the fact that the spiritual world is always willing to connect with you.

Casting a Circle

Before you perform a spell, you can cast a circle to increase its power. If you're outside, mark it in the ground. Inside, you can use a piece of string, paint, chalk or objects in a circle. A good size is 9 feet in diameter, but do what fits your space and needs.

If you're spell-casting with others, bring them into the circle before you cast it. Then, you can either walk the perimeter of the circle in small steps, or point at the perimeter of the circle with your finger, a stick, or a wand, and turn in a circle. Either way you choose, outline the circle three times. If you use a special name for yourself when making magic, repeat that name to yourself as you outline the circle. Or, you can repeat something like *We join together* if you are with friends. Envision a wall of energy extending up from the sides of the circle, protecting you and everything inside of it and concentrating your power. When you have finished with your spell, envision that these walls have now extended to infinity, and then imagine them flattening down to spread the magic you have created throughout the world. Leave the circle together and take any candles or other instruments of magic with you.

Writing Your Own Spells

After you've become comfortable performing some of the spells and charms in this book, feel free to expand your skills by conjuring up your own. In the back of this book, you'll find colors, stones, flowers, herbs, essential oils, and even birds that are special to love magic. Use them—along with the moon phases and lucky days listed—to create your own rituals that hold meaning for you. As for what to say, start with nothing, and see if any words come to you. You may find yourself saying something repetitive over and over. Try chanting it rhythmically in a way that feels good to you.

Or, if you want to write something in advance, speak it aloud as your write to make sure it has a natural feeling. Try to employ rhyme to make it even more soothing and natural. Take a notepad with you to write down thoughts as they come—natural paper and a neutral ink like blue work better than using your phone to write things in. You may be surprised at what surfaces where.

The Tools of Love Magic

A smudge stick is a bundle of sage (and other herbs, if you desire—see page 234). To make a smudge stick, dry the herbs and then tie them with twine or another natural rope to a stick. After lighting it on fire, blow it out so it smokes like incense. Then place it in a bowl or use it to smudge an area (see page 4).

PEN AND INK

The instruments one uses to complete spells are of the utmost importance. Using an old pen is better than a new one—any pen that has meaning to you is preferable to a cheap one you just bought at the drugstore. For best results, use a quill (especially one you made yourself) and ink. No matter what the instrument, using blue ink is good for neutrality, but red is often good for love spells. Take a look at the list of colors on page 230 for the best ink to write your spell in, if it's not already specified.

CANDLES

Candles are an important part of magic. Light them with a natural wood match, and use a candle in a color that corresponds to the results you want to achieve. Pink or red are good for love, while black can be useful when ending a relationship. Candle colors are often specified when used in spells in this book, but for more options, see the color list on page 230. Make sure to be careful around fire. Candles should only be used by adults and should never be left unattended.

SACHETS AND RIBBONS

You'll find several spells in this book contain sachets, or pouches for magical items. Sachets are best made out of natural material like cotton, leather, or silk. Make sure they're clean before you use them, and haven't been exposed to any bad energies (smudge them to be safe). You can make your own sachets by simply tying up the corners of a piece of cloth and tying with a natural thread, yarn, or ribbon. Ribbons, cords, and even ropes are often used on their own in spells for their powerful symbolism.

ROSEWATER

Sort of like a holy water for love, you can use rosewater to give yourself good luck in love and passion in any situation. It's also used specifically in some of the spells in this book. To make it, gather six roses: red for romantic love, pink for loyalty and friendship, and/or white for peace and harmony. Place a pot of 2 quarts of water over medium heat. Take each rose and peel one petal off at a time, letting it fall into the water. As you do, think loving or romantic thoughts. They can be about one specific person, or many people. Once the water starts to simmer, lower the heat and cover. After 30 minutes, when the pink and red petals have lost most of their color, turn off and let cool. Then remove the petals and bury them. Dilute the mixture by half with more water.

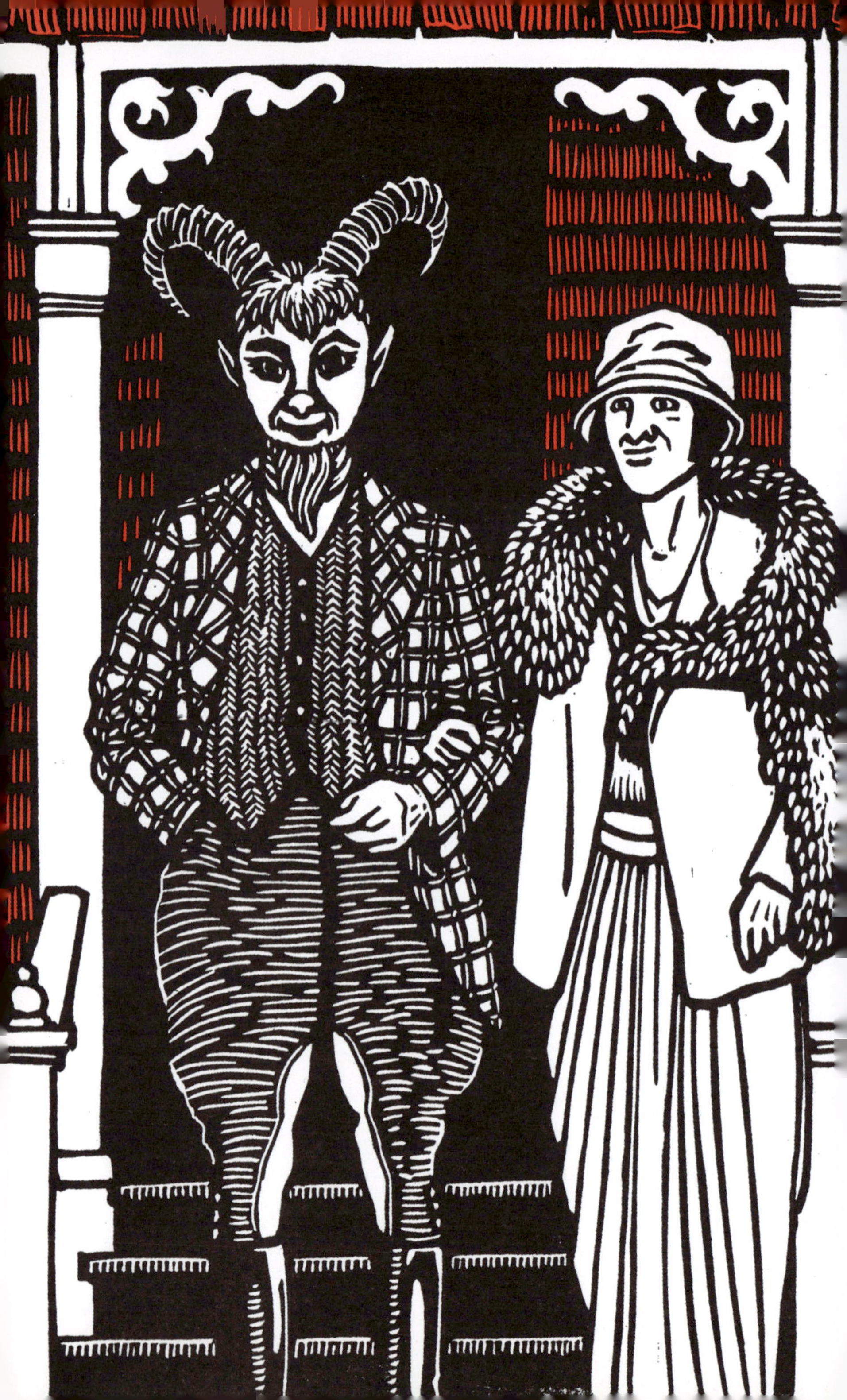

PLATONIC LOVE AND ANIMAL FRIENDS

FRIENDSHIP POTION
ANASTASIA GREYWOLF

To make people more open to becoming friends with you and to strengthen existing friendships, drink this potion. Put rose quartz in water for seven hours, then remove it. Drink the water before seeing your friend or your desired friend.

FOR BRINGING OLD FRIENDS TOGETHER
JILL ROBI

If you've lost touch with or feel distant from an old friend, take an image of them and write on the back of it how you feel about them and how much you miss them. As you seal the picture in a blue envelope, chant three times: *My emotions are bare. Answer and return.* Mail the picture to yourself, repeating the chant once a day before you go to sleep until the envelope returns to you. When it arrives, read what you wrote about your friend, then call that person before twenty-four hours have passed.

TO RECONNECT WITH A LONG-LOST FRIEND
KATRIEL WINTERS

Light a blue, silver, or white candle. (If using a larger candle, this spell can be performed over a period of several days, relighting the candle each day.) Alternatively, use a sticky note and write down your petition about your relationship, drawing a symbol of communication. Infuse it with intent. No matter which option you choose, say:

> *May my message of peace and friendship*
> *fly on swift wings.*

SISTERHOOD SPELL FOR FEMALE FRIENDS
SUSAN ADCOX

One can never have too many sisters of the heart. Use this spell if you have an acquaintance or casual friend who you would like to know better. Burn a candle to make your relationship "wax" or grow. A white candle will help the two of you connect on a higher plane. Since silver is associated with the moon, a symbol of womanhood, you may want to hold or wear a piece of silver jewelry when you recite the spell:

Bound by choice and not by blood,
Be for me a sister good.
Share the joy, halve the pain,
Our love will ever wax, not wane.

TALISMAN FOR LONG-DISTANCE FRIENDS
JEANNE DE LA WARE

Traditionally, seven cloves were worn in a bag on the body as a charm for friendship. The crocus flower, with its teardrop-shaped petals, is also an ancient symbol of friendship—particularly for visiting a faraway friend. Additionally, its violet color is associated with friendship.

To create this talisman you will need two small pieces of violet fabric or paper, scissors, clove oil, and a dropper. Cut two teardrop shapes out of your purple cloth or paper. Recite the following while touching the clove oil to each teardrop seven times. Give or send one to your faraway friend.

Seven clove drops for
delight in each other's company,
mutual support and help,
seeing and understanding each other truly,
loyalty,
equality between friends,
wishes for the other's well-being,

> *and the strength of the friendship even in absence.*
> *As hardy crocuses grow in all climates and bloom in dark seasons,*
> *so shall our friendship remain strong no matter where we are.*

TO MAKE FRIENDS WHILE YOU TRAVEL
THOMAS JENKINS

Travel can be lonely. This spell will open you up to new people when you are far from home. Before leaving on your journey, pour a small amount of lavender oil in a bowl. Light a candle and recite:

> *I am never far from home, for I am always with Mother Earth. As I travel, please open my mind to new experiences, my eyes to new truths, and my heart to new people. May I be an ambassador for myself, shunning fear and embracing the love in the hearts of others. The world contains my brothers and sisters, my friends and lovers, and wisdom to be shared as well as stories to be created. I seek this and so I shall find it.*

Blow out the candle. Pour the oil in a container, and apply a few drops before going out when you travel.

LOVE MAGIC

NEW TOWN FRIENDSHIP TREE CHARM
ANASTASIA GREYWOLF

If you've moved to a new city or town, use this charm to bring friends into your life. Gather some strands of rib-

PLATONIC LOVE AND ANIMAL FRIENDS

bon. They can all look the same, but it's better if they have varying colors, lengths, and textures to represent the different kinds of friends you want in your life. Tie each one to a different tree where you would like to meet new friends.

TO BRING PEOPLE WITH SIMILAR INTERESTS INTO YOUR LIFE
GRETA GOLDBART

Gather together basil leaves, sliced ginger root, a mortar and pestle, a small jar or Tupperware container, and a mirror.

Crush a few basil leaves and a small amount of ginger root in a mortar and pestle until well mixed and paste-like. Place the mixture in the small container, and refrigerate overnight to allow the components to combine their energy and power. The next day, set a small mirror up in a plot of earth around your home. Bury the mixture in front of the mirror so that you can see yourself performing the act. The components, charged with attractive energies, will take in the power of your reflection and summon similar people into your life.

FRIENDSHIP OIL
GABRIEL GREY

Make this oil blend and apply it when you find yourself in a situation to make a new friend.

- ¼ cup avocado oil
- 3 drops rose essential oil
- 1 drop bergamot essential oil

Mix together while thinking good intentions for the friendship. Place a few drops on your skin before meeting new acquaintances.

TO BRING HELP IN TIMES OF NEED
ANASTASIA GREYWOLF

To bring someone into your life when you're in a time of need, place seven coriander seeds in a black sachet with a white flower. Put that sachet in a red or pink sachet and place it in a box made of a natural material like wood or cardboard. Bury the box in your yard or somewhere meaningful to you. When you're going through a challenging time, unearth the box and take out one of the seeds. Replace the flower and bury the box in a new location. Then plant the coriander seed close to the surface of wet soil somewhere that has significance to the problem you're experiencing. Someone who can be trusted will come into your life to help you through the time of need. When you run out of seeds, repeat the process.

PERFECT PARTY POUCHES
SAVANA LEE

Conversation is flowing, good energy is growing, and friendships that last a lifetime are forming—for the devoted party host or hostess, here's a potion pouch to harness the energies of communication, entertainment, and connection. It's recommended you make at least one pouch for every room your guests will be spending time in. This potion caters to the creativity of the host/hostess. If your party is seasonal or for a holiday, for example, feel to add in color (dried fruit or herbs) and essential oil scents that are relevant, such as cranberry, pine, or juniper for Christmas, or orange, licorice, and cherry for Halloween. For a basic pouch, you will need:

> 1 teaspoon lemon zest and 2 drops lemon essential oil—to invite clarity, joy, and a fresh sense of adventure
>
> ¼ cup fresh or dried rosemary—a traditional herb for friendship and remembrance
>
> ½ cup dried lavender and 1 drop lavender essential oil (optional)—to calm your guests and ease any fear of meeting new people

PLATONIC LOVE AND ANIMAL FRIENDS

¼ cup dried rose hips—to help foster love toward one another

½ tablespoon salt—for the strength of the earth and good boundaries

You will also need small bags; use something thin and breathable. Mesh or knit bags are fine as long as your mixture won't fall out. If you wish you can tie the bags with a piece of colored silk for more beauty and to help your party flow smoothly.

To prepare the bags, light a candle (preferably one you will light at the party) and place it on your left. In a large bowl, mix all the dry ingredients with a spoon. If you are using any holiday ingredients, add them at this time.

On small pieces of paper, one for each pouch, write a word you would like to infuse into your party atmosphere. Some suggestions: *playful, fun, connection, friendship, joy,* and *amusement.* When done, set them around the bowl in a clockwise circle and recite the following spell aloud:

> *I call into being a perfect setting for connection, vivacity, joy, and friendship. Let this salt call the strength of the Earth so all may feel safe here. Let the lemon lift our spirits, the lavender calm us, and the rosemary remind us to always see the good in one another. May the spirit of these words call forth the essence of each; may they find their highest expression here.*

Add your essential oils to the mix, stirring until the oil is evenly distributed. Finish the potion with these words:

> *I bless these pouches with these oils. May they allow us to bring our highest selves to this space and connect with open minds and hearts. Bless this space and all who attend. So mote it be.*

Using a spoon, divide your mixture evenly among the bags and add one of the papers from your circle into each bag.

After you finish the pouches, you can set out them out next to oil diffusers for stronger scents or even send them home with your guests as party favors to keep the good energy flowing. These pouches go great on plants, above doorways, or set out with your household decorations to radiate welcoming energies to your guests.

BLESSING FOR A NEW FRIENDSHIP
ELISA SHOENBERGER

This spell is intended for the beginning of a new friendship. Ideally, it should be performed after your first substantive meeting, such as a coffee outing or dinner. You'll need a sprig of Alstroemeria, a yellow rose, a glass of red wine, and a small sachet. (If Alstroemeria is not available, substitute a second yellow rose.) Perform the spell as the sun is rising a few days after you begin your new friendship. Make sure you have clear access to the sun's rays.

Place the Alstroemeria on a flat, sunlit surface. Take the yellow rose and place it on top of the Alstroemeria so that the two flowers form an *X* or two crossing arrows. Fill a small glass with the wine and place a petal of each flower inside the wine. Chant:

> *As two arrows crossed in flight*
> *Make this new friendship bright*
> *Embrace this blossoming new rapport*
> *With kindness and sweetness evermore.*

Let the flowers dry out in the sun. When they have completely dried, take a petal from each and place it in the sachet. Keep the sachet in your bag or purse for the first few months of the new friendship.

TO SPREAD LOVE TO FRIENDS
ANASTASIA GREYWOLF

If you'd like to send a loving spirit to friends, join together with other like-minded friends and perform this ritual. Light three candles: one white, one pink, and one yellow. Write the names of people who need love on white paper with blue ink. Place the candles in a triangle formation, then place the pieces of paper in the middle of the

LOVE MAGIC

candles. Sprinkle pink rose petals over the piece of paper. Hold hands with the others and focus positive energy and good intentions toward the middle of the circle. You may even want to make a humming sound together to help focus the energy even more.

TO MAKE A FRIEND FALL IN LOVE WITH YOU
SUZANNE LAREAU

The advantage of working a love spell on a friend is that the person already knows and likes you—you have a running start. But consider well whether you truly want to alter your relationship, and remember that with this spell you are influencing the energy in your favor, but you cannot make a person do something against their will (nor should you want to!). To increase this spell's power, cast it on a Friday, preferably at the full moon or during the waxing moon.

Take a small personal object belonging to your friend—a piece of jewelry, an item of clothing, or a handwritten note the person wrote—and drip three drops of rose oil on the object. Tie and knot a narrow yellow ribbon around the object. Next, wrap a wide red ribbon over the narrow ribbon, obscuring the yellow; tie a knot on the opposite side of the object from the yellow knot. (If the object is too difficult to wrap in this way, drop it into a small muslin bag and wrap the bag.) As you do this, visualize a rosebud ripening into a full-blown red rose and say: *Like the bud that blooms in its time, let our friendship ripen to love.* Place the object under your pillow for three nights; each night before sleep, hold the object in your hand and repeat the incantation.

TO MAKE A FRIEND FALL OUT OF LOVE WITH YOU

SUZANNE LAREAU

It happens to all of us—a friend sees you as more than a friend, but you don't share those feelings. Intended to cool unrequited love while preserving the friendship, this spell is most effective when performed during the waning moon. Write the name of the person whose passions you wish to chill on a small strip of parchment or organic paper. Use a pencil, so there is no ink to run and the name remains legible when the paper is wet. Fold the paper into thirds and then wrap it with a length of white ribbon or embroidery thread, tying the thread in a tight knot. As you bind the paper, focus your intention on restricting the love your friend feels for you to the love of pure friendship.

Fill a small plastic container with a tight-fitting lid about a third full of water. Immerse the bound name in the water until the small packet is thoroughly saturated. Weight the paper with a turquoise stone, used to align friendship. These gestures will dampen your friend's romantic love for you and ensure that your friendship takes priority. Seal the container and place it in the back of your freezer; leave it in place until you are confident that your friendship is on firm ground and the infatuation your friend felt for you has passed.

TO KEEP YOURSELF FROM FALLING IN LOVE WITH YOUR FRIEND
AOIFE WITT

If you find you're falling for a friend and you know you shouldn't, find a long piece of string. Any string, yarn, or ribbon will do, but grey string is the best because grey is a passion-dampening color. The string should be long enough for you to make several knots in it. Choose a time when you won't be disturbed, and sit with the string in your lap. Imagine your friend and commit to perfect honesty with yourself, because you're now going to envision an entire romantic relationship with your friend—good *and* bad. Allow yourself to imagine what it would be like to start a relationship with them. For each milestone in the relationship, make a knot in your thread: first kiss, first date, first time you have sex. As you make your knots, include the bad things that would happen too: the first time they don't text you back, your friendship turning awkward, your breakup, and finally the loss of your friendship. Picture it all in detail. Live it as much as possible, and put all that emotion into each knot.

When you have made your final knot, keep the string as a charm. You can carry it with you, or hang it somewhere you will see it every day. When the feelings for your friend fade, you can dispose of it.

TO SILENCE GOSSIP
TRADITIONAL

To banish gossip among friends, explain as concisely as possible on a piece of parchment paper what matter you need the spirits' help in silencing. Place this paper inside a small glass. Place a single sliver of ice on top of the paper, then break an egg (use white eggs only, not brown) over the ice. Bury as far away as possible.

TO KEEP FRIENDS OR RELATIVES FROM GETTING JEALOUS
JILL ROBI

Take an image of yourself and an image of your jealous friend or relative and place them back to back. Bind the two images with a yellow ribbon at least twelve inches long. Once it is completely wrapped, hold the image over sage smoke and chant the following for a full minute:

> *You will see me, positively.*
> *Negative out, positive in.*

FOR CURING JEALOUS FEELINGS TOWARD YOUR FRIEND
JILL ROBI

If you feel yourself having jealous feelings toward a friend, you can help assuage them with this sachet.

Take a piece of turquoise, a stick of cinnamon, and a sprig each of thyme, rosemary, and lemongrass. Place them into a green sachet. Be sure to carry this with you whenever you see the friend you are jealous of, and think positive thoughts for them and for yourself.

BAD ENERGY CLEANSE BEFORE GIVING ADVICE
LUNA ETERNAL

To cleanse the mind and home of negative energy so that you can give good advice to loved ones in need, gather a bundle of dried sage, a white feather, a broom, and enough salt to cover all of the entrances of your home. Open all the doors and windows, and focus your will on what you want. Place the broom at your front door. Starting at the back of your home, light the sage, and with the feather, spread the smoke around the room, moving first in the direction of the windows. Use a sweeping motion to direct the smoke out of the windows. Once at the window, spread the salt in a line on the sill and close the window. Repeat the process in each room of your home, working your way to the front door. Spread salt on the threshold and close the door. Once outside, perform the ritual at each corner of your property to ensure the bad energy cannot return. Before you enter your home again, wave the sage bundle over yourself to cleanse yourself of any negative energy that may be clinging to you, starting at your feet and working your way up. Use a sweeping motion away from your body. Finally, use the broom to sweep out any negative energy that may be trailing you. Let the sage continue to burn down. You and your home should be free of any negative influences or energy!

TO PREVENT FIGHTS WITH FRIENDS
M. D. MCDUFF

Here is a potion to make and a spell to cast to help maintain harmony and peace within a group of friends and prevent fighting and strife. You will need:

1 sage stick

1 coconut

A hammer and nail

Blueberries

Raspberries

1 peach

1 lemon

PLATONIC LOVE AND ANIMAL FRIENDS

1 lime
1 mint sprig
1 geranium plant
Honeysuckle petals
1 tablespoon witch hazel
1 tablespoon aloe

In the place where you will be preparing the potion, burn sage to ensure protection and promote longevity and positive wishes.

Use the nail to hammer a hole into the end of a coconut. The coconut channels protection for your relationships with your friends. Pour the coconut water into a container and set aside.

Crack open the coconut so that you can use at least part of it as a bowl. If your coconut bowl is too shallow, take a utensil and dig out some of the meat from the center so that it can hold your ingredients.

Add blueberries and raspberries for protection again strife. Dice a peach into small pieces and add them to the berries for positive intentions and the longevity of friendship.

Cut a lemon in half and squeeze it over the fruit to promote love and friendship; do the same with a lime for love and healing. Add a mint spring for strength.

Use a small spoon to crush the fruit, then add in a small portion of the reserved coconut water. While you stir, speak the name of your friends, including your own name. Repeat for the entire time that you stir. When thoroughly mixed, drink this concoction.

To complete the circle of protection, pluck the petals of one geranium, which represents genuine friendship. Place the petals in the same coconut bowl you drank from, along with the honeysuckle petals for protection. Pour in the witch hazel and aloe, also for protection. Stir your concoction. While stirring, again speak the names of your friends, including your name. Repeat while stirring. When finished, take your coconut bowl and concoction outside, if you're not there already. Face the east and speak these words:

> *Should conflict seep within our ties*
> *Taking on a stealthy guise*
> *Hear our voices, hear our cries*
> *Cast it out, up to the skies*

Throw the coconut into the air, aiming toward the east. Wherever it falls, let it lie.

TO BRING LOVE BACK INTO A FRIENDSHIP
KATRIEL WINTERS

This spell is to be used when a friendship has gone cold. Find a tea light or votive candle. (If using a votive or larger candle, the spell can be repeated over a period of several days.) A blue or purple candle is preferred, but white or ivory will work fine too. Light the candle and say the person's name. Recite: *I wish for the best between us and the warmth of friendship.* Imagine a winter—like chill slowly melting to reveal the growth of spring buds.

TO FORGIVE FRIENDS
JILL ROBI

Take black, brown, blue, or clear sardonyx stones (or preferably a mixture of all four if you can manage), and place them into a small leather sachet with sweet fennel, dill leaves, and patchouli leaves. Carry the sachet with you to dispel the hurt caused by a dear friend who has wronged you.

TO GET ALONG WITH A ROOMMATE
ANASTASIA GREYWOLF

Place a photo of yourself, a photo of your roommate, a leaf of sage, and a pearl in front of a lit pink candle. Take a rope, cut it in half, and say: *Though we are separate, we can come together.* Tie the rope back together and place it between the photographs. Think positive thoughts about your roommate while the candle burns. When it burns out, place the sachet in a drawer in your home, or bury it in a potted plant. Your relationship will improve.

TO EASE ANXIETY IN SOCIAL SITUATIONS
SUSAN ADCOX

Many people struggle with social anxiety, and most people experience it at one time or another. If you find yourself tense and worried before you are supposed to spend time with others, find a quiet corner and create a calming spot. Drink chamomile tea, breathe in the fragrance of a sprig of rosemary, or simply do some deep breathing. Then repeat this spell:

> *Grant me confidence and grace.*
> *All misgivings be erased.*
> *Make of this time a charmed space*
> *In which good things proceed apace.*

TO EASE TENSION IN A FRIENDSHIP
GRETA GOLDBART

For this charm you will need:

> 1 strip of paper
> Your favorite writing utensil
> Eucalyptus essential oil
> 1 jar with a lid
> 1 small candle
> Dried yellow rosebuds.

On a cloudy day, write down your name and your friend's name on the strip of paper, along with a brief description of the source of the tension. Sprinkle a few drops of eucalyptus oil onto the paper and fold it half. Place it in a jar along with the small candle and several dried yellow rosebuds or a handful of the petals. (Make sure they are completely dry to prevent mold from growing in the jar!) Wait about a week for a day when the sky is completely clear. Open the jar, sprinkle the rose petals outside your door, and remove the candle. Place it in an appropriate holder and light it. Burn the piece of paper in the flame of the candle, and let the candle burn completely. Conclude by speaking aloud this affirmation:

> *Tension slackens to a relaxed position,*
> *Friendship is stronger than opposition.*

TO HEAL A RIFT BETWEEN BEST FRIENDS
GRETA GOLDBART

For this spell, you'll need a small piece of paper and a pen, a length of string or cord, scissors, and a matchbook or lighter.

On the paper, write a short description or word that summarizes the disagreement or reason for the rift between you and your best friend. Place the length of cord on top of the paper, and cut it in half. Burn the paper and tie the string back together with a simple knot between the cut ends, then tie the entire cord around your wrist. Wear it until the friendship is healed.

FOR GOOD TIMES WITH FRIENDS
SUSAN ADCOX

Nothing nurtures the soul like being with friends. Even with good friends though, that feeling of connectedness doesn't always happen. Use this spell to avoid awkwardness and achieve the friendly union that your spirit needs. Orange and yellow are warm, sociable colors, so burn candles in those colors, or hold a piece of topaz, citrine, or amber when you recite this spell.

I need a night . . .

When laughter is easy
And tension is banned.
When happiness seems
Ours to command.

Give me a night . . .

With my familiars, my friends
Who make my heart whole,
Who lighten my burden
And give peace to my soul.

FOR PEACE AND COMMUNICATION BETWEEN ALL CREATURES
SAVANA LEE

This spell will bring peace and open communication to all creatures in your home, whether furred, feathered, clawed, or winged, from land or sea. Perform it either the night of or the night after the full moon.

You will need a sage smudge stick (see page 7), small white cloths that contain the scent of each creature you wish to include in the magic (you can pet them with the cloth to obtain the scent), a white candle, a small amount of earth from the area surrounding the house, a small cup of purified water (set out by the light of the full moon for extra potency to absorb energies of potential and Mother

Nature's nurturing abundance), and a rubber band or string of your choice.

To begin, light the sage stick and smudge both your body and the white cloths by wafting the smoke from the sage from left to right. Light the white candle and lay the cloths with the animal scents next to each other. Recite these words aloud:

> *I call on Mother Nature and the elements of the world: Earth, Fire, Water, and Air. I call on the Earth to help me ground this home and make a peaceful foundation for all who live here. I call on Fire to cleanse this house of any negativity and burn away the past until all is clean and forgiven. I call on Water to cleanse our energies and the nurturing light of the Full Moon's energies to bring about our fullest natures. I call on Air to carry the intentions of communication and peace. I allow our energies to be bound in connection and joy.*

Pass each cloth over the candle without letting it touch the flame. Set it down and sprinkle it lightly with a dusting of earth and a few drops of water. Repeat with each cloth. Lay the cloths on top of each other. Fold them in half and in half again. As you secure them with your chosen string, recite the following words aloud to bind the spell:

*All in this house are connected by respect and love.
The lines of communication are open and flowing.
Our energies mix well and we are bound by nature
and family. May these animals rooted in the elements
communicate their needs to each other and to me in an
easy peaceful manner. So mote it be.*

Leave the cloths bound for twenty-four hours per cloth or creature in the house. After that you may dispose of them as you like and find your flow in connection and trust.

TO GET PETS TO LOVE EACH OTHER
SUSAN ADCOX

Pets that quarrel are a worry for their owners. If your pets don't get along, use this spell. Find a quiet place to cast it, and hold each pet in turn while you recite the words. You can finish the spell by placing a drop of water or olive oil on your pet's head. (Essential oils can be toxic to pets and should not be used.) You can also finish the spell by giving your pet a small treat. To personalize the spell, replace the first words of the spell with the names of your pets or otherwise alter the first line to fit your situation.

*Canine, feline, friends of mine,
Let your actions be divine.
No more pain from teeth or claws,
Only peace from head to paws.*

LOVE MAGIC

TO GET YOUR PET TO LIKE YOUR SIGNIFICANT OTHER
KATRIEL WINTERS

Pets have a heightened sense of smell and will often warn of danger to their humans. But for those who are shy or skittish, or want to know if their pet is comfortable around their partner, try this spell.

Situate your animal near your significant other, maintaining a distance of about two feet. Your partner should not look the animal in the eyes, but should hold a hand out. Maintain this position. If you are doing this spell by yourself, borrow some item of your partner's and put it near, but not in, your pet's preferred bed. Say: *[Your pet's name], I wish you to be as comfortable with this person as I am with them.* Give your pet a treat.

TO COMPEL AN ANIMAL TO FOLLOW YOU
TRADITIONAL

To compel a dog, horse, or other animal to follow you, utter these words three times into its right ear:

> *Casper guide thee, Balthazar bind thee,*
> *Melchior keep thee.*

CAT AND DOG FRIENDSHIP SPELL
CALYX REED

This spell will unite your feuding cat and dog and help them see eye-to-eye and paw-to-paw. Recite this incantation at nine in the evening in a subtly lit room with the shades drawn and two small plates of catnip and peanut butter laid out before your animals.

An autumn's eve falls yet again,
and my two best will become friends.
Though fur and species difference
has made my pets indifferent
to friendship and to harmony
catnip and peanut butter both agree
that with a simple whiff of both
under each one's furry nose,
at nine p.m. when the time's right,
they will unite within my sight.
I'll pet them both so gently that
they'll have no choice but to resolve their spat.
A cat's a cat, a dog's a dog,
but underneath a scented fog
of tasty treats and loving words
there will be no anger heard.

LOVE POTION FOR DOGS
GEMMA ARONSON

This love potion will help your dog love you and be loyal only to you. It will work during a waxing moon, but a full moon will make it stronger. You will need:

  3 teaspoons of rainwater

  Chalice

  Mortar and pestle

  2 coriander seeds

1 hair from your head
Cotton cloth for straining.

Place the rainwater in your chalice. Using the mortar and pestle, grind the coriander seeds as you chant the following:

Seeds from my heart
Bind us together
Never apart

Add two pinches of the ground seeds to the rainwater. Add your hair to your chalice. Now chant the following to bind the spell:

My body I give
Love won't be broken
Whilst we both live

Let that soak until the rise of the sun. Strain the potion and stir it well into your dog's breakfast as you whisper your dog's name seven times.

CAT LOVE SPELL
GEMMA ARONSON

We all know how aloof cats are; you're the love of their life when they're hungry and you're just an annoying roommate when they're full. This love spell will help your cat realize that he or she needs your affections always and forever. Perform this spell under a full moon. You will need:

> 1 red candle
> 1 red cloth (in cotton, linen, or silk)
> Rose quartz
> 3 apple seeds
> 2 basil leaves,
> Cotton string or natural twine.

Light your candle and lay the red cloth down. Pass the rose quartz over the flame of the candle two times, and place the crystal on the cloth. Hold the apple seeds in your left hand and chant:

> *With these seeds from the fruit of love*
> *Under the full moon up above*
> *Take these and bind our love*

Put the seeds on the cloth next to the crystal. Now place the basil leaves in your left hand. Close your eyes and say your cat's name three times to bind the spell. Place the leaves on top of the crystal. Pull the four corners of the red cloth together—with the crystal, seeds, and basil inside—to form a small charm pouch. Tie the pouch together with the string by winding it three times around. Tie it with two knots and chant:

PLATONIC LOVE AND ANIMAL FRIENDS

Let your love be
You and me
So mote it be

Place the charm pouch in your cat's bed or sleeping place.

TO ATTRACT A SKITTISH ANIMAL
AOIFE WITT

This practice is for winning the affections of a skittish or standoffish animal, like a feral cat. Important note: If you have an animal that might be dangerous, like a frightened dog, do not do this. Call your vet or animal trainer!

While nothing works better than patience and treats when getting an animal to love you, a little magic never hurts. Like many creatures, pets are drawn to energy.

If you have an aloof animal, sit down and meditate in the area where the animal lives. Face away from it. Don't pay it any attention at all. Just pay attention to your breathing. Feel your body in the space. Clear your mind.

Once you're relaxed, feel around for the pet's energy. Can you hear the pet? Can you feel its energy? Focus on it. With your mind, reach out to the pet. You might, for example, imagine yourself getting up, going to the animal, and petting it. You might reach out telepathically. Or you might just sit there, observing the pet's presence. At the end, get up and leave the room. (It's a good idea to leave a treat as a thank you.)

Repeat this exercise at regular intervals. Eventually, if the animal is free to come over to you, it should begin to approach. Continue this meditation until the animal is comfortable with you and you can begin your friendship.

TO ADOPT THE RIGHT CAT OR DOG FOR YOU
GRETA GOLDBART

Substitution: If you are a regular magic practitioner, you can instead conduct small rituals near the animal, casting a big enough circle so that the animal doesn't cross the boundary.

TO ADOPT THE RIGHT CAT OR DOG FOR YOU
GRETA GOLDBART

For this spell, you'll need two crystals or stones. Rose quartz, a beautiful pink stone with ties to love, emotional connection, and friendship, is ideal, but any stone that resonates with you will do. Sleep with one stone under your pillow for a week at least, a full moon cycle if you can, to charge it with your energy. Set the other stone aside, and do not charge it. Go to the adoption center and meet a few potential furry friends. Spend some one-on-one time with each animal. Then, present the two stones concealed, one in each fist. If the animal is attracted to the stone you charged, you have a strongly compatible energy. Of course, there are many other factors involved in choosing the right friend for you, but this is a good way to get a feeling for the energy of a potential cat or dog pal.

TO CHARM A SNAKE
LAUREN RODINO

A snake's loyalty may be hard to win, but it is well worth the effort. At three a.m. on the night of a blue moon, stir together the following mixture: vinegar, the brain of a rat, the leg of a toad, a picture of Cleopatra, and an emerald crystal. Let the mixture soak.

At the end of one month, recite the following spell: *Regius Anguis, Atheris Squamigera. O mighty basilisk, let me be one with your kind.* Keep the crystal in your pocket for whenever the snake's devotion is required.

TO GET A HORSE TO LOVE YOU
GEMMA ARONSON

This powerful spell will enable your horse's heart to fall in love with you. It will take effect in a week and will be stronger if started on the first quarter of the moon's cycle. You will need:

>1 pink or red candle
>   (with at least an eight-hour burn time)
>
>1 knife
>
>1 deep red apple
>
>2 teaspoons of sugar
>
>Parchment or organic paper
>
>1 white cotton or linen cloth
>
>1 fresh rosemary sprig
>
>Red string or wool.

Start by lighting your candle. Using the knife, cut the apple from top to bottom into two equal halves. Pick out the seeds. Each half represents your two hearts. Sprinkle the sugar equally into each hollow where the seeds were and chant:

> *With these sweet apple halves*
> *I will to bond our hearts*
> *Never let us be apart*

Write your horse's name on the piece of parchment, fold it carefully in one of the apple hollows, then close the apple. Wrap the apple in the cloth and place the rosemary sprig on the bundle. Bind the bundle and rosemary together with the string by wrapping it eight times. Tie the bundle in a double knot. Seal the knot with three drops of melted wax from your candle. Blow out your candle.

At dawn, bury your bundle at the foot of a beech or chestnut tree. Light your candle for one hour every night for seven nights, or until the moon is at its fullest.

TO TALK TO BIRDS
TRADITIONAL

Take the tongue of a vulture and lay it for three days and three nights in honey, afterward under your tongue. Thusly, you will understand all the songs of birds.

TO COMMUNICATE WITH ANIMALS WITH YOUR MIND
ANASTASIA GREYWOLF

To commune with an animal you have a relationship with, look into its eyes while envisioning a light encircling you both. Close your eyes, match the rhythm of your breathing to the animal, and think:

> *I pronounce to thee my intentions,*
> *with heart and spirit high.*

> *I am here to hear, or to be.*
> *Be my animal guide.*

Be aware of any message the animal may be sending.

TO TRANSFORM AN ANIMAL INTO A HUMAN
CALYX REED

If your best animal pal is missing out on your human adventures, repeat this spell to them at a time when you are both sitting on the front step of your home, facing your future together.

> *My furry friend you've been so good.*
> *Accompanied me just where you could.*
> *But alas you cannot go*
> *To supermarkets or to a show.*
> *So with this new and secret spell*
> *I'll make our situation swell.*
> *From animal to human pal*
> *I change your form and love you well.*
> *As a person you can find*
> *Adventures hidden to animal kind.*
> *Your disposition will remain*
> *Though your form won't be the same.*
> *We'll have fun together here*
> *As humans! Yes, indeed, as peers!*

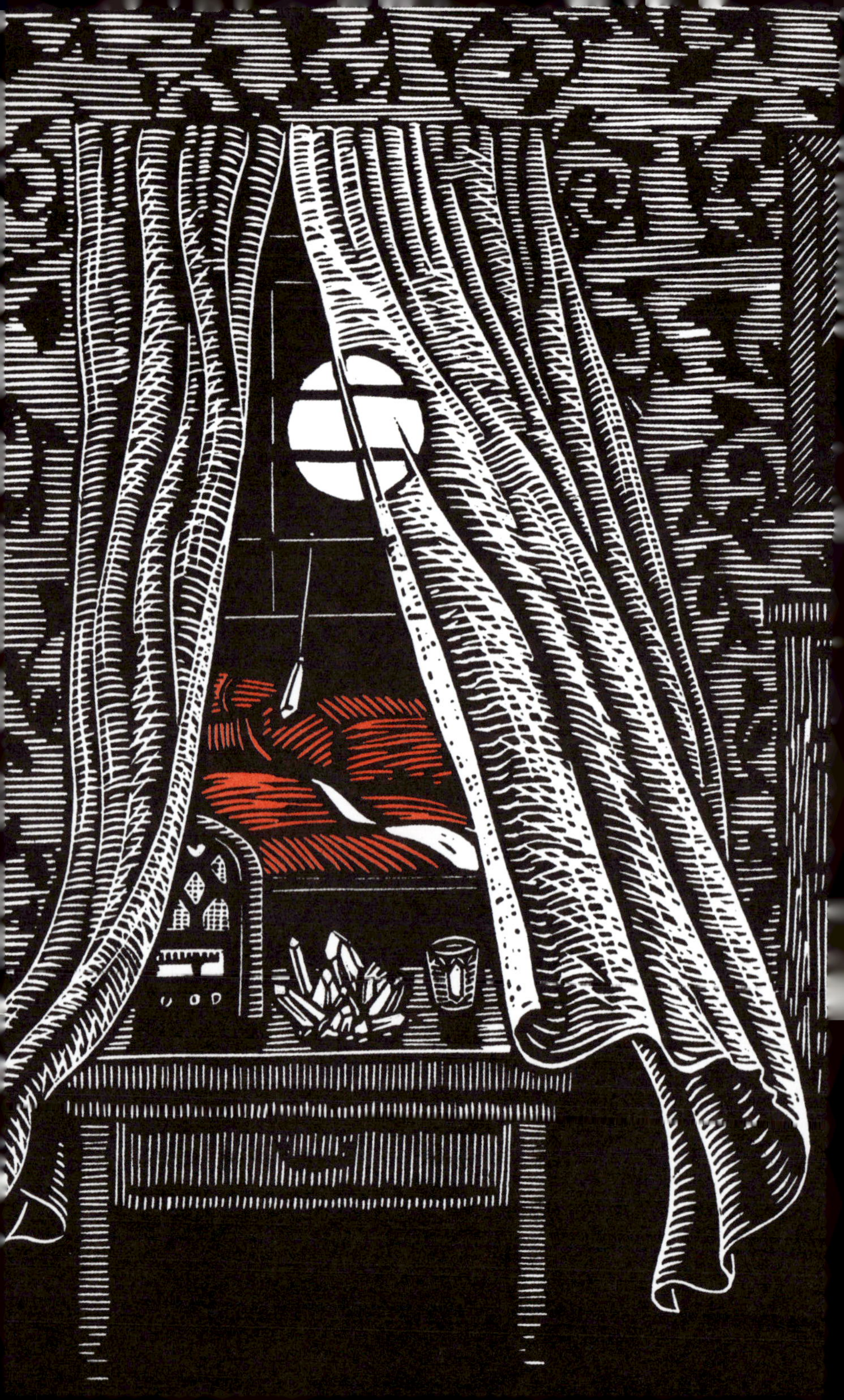

DATING AND FINDING LOVE

SPELL TO WELCOME LOVE
THOMAS JENKINS

Sometimes we just need to prepare ourselves to receive love. This simple incantation is useful to recite before a date or while getting over a bad breakup:

> *I am a child of the universe. I am worthy of love. I open myself to love so that it may enter my heart. I will extend myself the love I wish to receive from the world. Shield my heart from those that would use it for evil, but always allow it to be open to those who come seeking with compassion.*

TO OPEN YOURSELF UP TO LOVE
ANASTASIA GREYWOLF

Place two walnuts in front of a scented pink or red candle. Surround yourself and the candle with fragrant flowers. Sit quietly and breathe in the scent while reciting:

> *Come to me, love,*
> *Come to me*
> *I am open*
> *I am free*
> *Come to me*
> *Come to me, love,*
> *I am waiting patiently.*

TO CURE SHYNESS
TRADITIONAL

If you suffer from shyness when talking to someone you're attracted to, use this charm to increase your self-confidence. Find a peacock feather and go to as open an area as possible, like a field. Holding one end, draw a heart in the air with the other end, repeating:

> *Tail feather*
> *Tail feather*
> *Wait and see*
> *Tail feather*
> *Tail feather*
> *I can be me*

SELF-CONFIDENCE CHARM
ANASTASIA GREYWOLF

Print out a photo of yourself and place it in a silver frame somewhere you'll see it daily. Before an occasion for which you need a boost of confidence, or on the night of a full moon, place items around your photo that evoke good memories or make you feel good about yourself—they can be photos of other friends, favorite books, or personal items. Play your favorite song and light some incense you enjoy. Light a white candle in front of the photo. Look into your own eyes and recite:

I release you
I release you
Here's the power
I release you

Then take a shower or bath and blow out the candle when you're done.

NAIL TRICK FOR LOVE
ANASTASIA GREYWOLF

Cut your nails on nine consecutive Sundays. Bury the clippings and you'll get the mate you've been wanting, or someone even better able to handle your faults.

BASIL SEED CHARM FOR LOVE
GABRIEL GREY

On the evening of a new moon, plant a basil seed while you think about your intended. Water the seed well to nurture it and help it germinate. As the basil plant sprouts and grows, harvest the leaves and make them into a tea that you sip as you focus your mental energy on your desired. Finally, pick the leaves from the same plant and cook them in a meal for your love.

ROSE PETAL LOVE CHARM
ANASTASIA GREYWOLF

Take eight roses—seven pink and one red. Give the seven pink ones to people who bring love and happiness into your home, visit frequently, or who possess positive energy. Take the petals from the red rose and sprinkle them over the pathway into your home. Don't remove them unless the rain has already washed them partially away. Make sure the object of your affection uses that pathway to enter your home. For extra effectiveness, have them walk over the petals soon after sprinkling them.

APPLE CHARM FOR ATTRACTING LOVE
TRADITIONAL

On three pieces of red or pink paper, write your name, your love's name, and your ardent wish for your love. On a Friday morning before sunrise, pick an apple from a tree. Cut it in half and remove the seeds, then place the notes in the middle. Tie it back together with twine and take it somewhere with good energy, like a location you enjoyed together. Untie the apple and eat half, then feed the other half to your love. Burn the notes.

WILLOW TREE CHARM
ANASTASIA GREYWOLF

If an unrequited love leaves their footprints in the earth, dig up the soil that held them and bury it under a willow tree. As you cover it, recite:

> *As you tread on earth*
> *Think of me*
> *As you tread on earth*
> *Come to me*
> *As you tread on earth*
> *Grow big and strong*
> *As you tread on earth*
> *A willow tree at dawn*

By the next morning, if it's meant to be, the person will start to fall in love with you.

CRYSTAL CHARM TO ATTRACT LOVE
TRADITIONAL

Take seven rose quartz stones and place them on a windowsill during a full moon for seven hours. Then, take each in your hand and recite a quality you would like your love to have. Keep the stones with you to attract love.

GARNET CHARM
GABRIEL GREY

Take two similar-looking pieces of garnet and carry them close together and close to yourself (like in your pocket) for a week. Then give one piece of garnet to the person you want to attract, or place it a backpack or something else they carry around often. The garnet you gave away will find its way back to the garnet you still possess.

TO MAKE YOURSELF FEEL ATTRACTIVE
ANASTASIA GREYWOLF

Be careful, this charm might also increase your fertility! In a white bowl, mash two strawberries and three raspberries with the juice of half of a lime, a spoonful of avocado oil, a drop of ylang-ylang essential oil, and a drop of jasmine essential oil. Mix in a spoonful of white sugar, then rub the mixture all over your body. Leave it on for as long as possible before washing it off.

FOR HEALING FROM A TROUBLED PAST
SUSAN ADCOX

Those who have experienced traumatic events may experience distress when bad memories surface. They need a short, simple spell that can be easily memorized. As an adjunct to the spell, they should carry a stone known for its healing qualities. Lapis lazuli and turquoise have healing powers, but a simple stone of polished agate can also be powerful. The stone should be kept in a purse or pocket so that it is close by when needed. Repeat:

> *Forget the past with torment fraught.*
> *Let bygone pains be forgot.*
> *Loosen now the hurting knot.*
> *Accept the love that fate has wrought.*

"NEVER FIND LOVE" REVERSAL CHARM
ANASTASIA GREYWOLF

Use this charm if you feel like you'll never find love. Place one drop of cedarwood essential oil and one drop of lemon essential oil on a piece of white paper. Write down one (and only one) negative word that you feel describes you. Burn the piece of paper over a black candle.

ANTI-NEGATIVITY BATH
ANASTASIA GREYWOLF

If you find yourself having negative thoughts or feelings about finding love, take this bath before you leave for a night out.

Place the petals of one dried red rose, one sprig of rosemary, and one sprig of marjoram in a sachet and run it under bath water. Add a drop of eucalyptus essential oil and a drop patchouli essential oil if you're especially looking for passion.

While bathing, think about all of your negativity drifting away.

TO BRING YOUR TRUE LOVE TO YOU
TRADITIONAL

To make your true love come into your life, eat an apple in front of a mirror. While you're eating it, recite:

> *Whoever my true love may be*
> *Come and eat this apple with me.*

TO MAKE LOVE FIND ITS WAY TO YOU
LUNA ETERNAL

Recite the following:

> *New moon hidden from sight*
> *Silver bowl to reflect love's light*
> *Rose quartz to attract love's kiss*
> *Red rose's passion to give its gift*
> *In the window to draw to me the man I will*
> > *So mote it be*

For this charm, you will need a silver bowl, a rose quartz stone, and rose petals (red or pink). Each line of the spell has a specific action you must perform during the ritual. Make sure this is done on the night of a new moon, so that the moon is hidden from sight. As you say, "Silver bowl to reflect love's light," hold the bowl up to the sky and then place it on the ground in front of you. Next, hold the rose quartz in your hand as you say, "Rose quartz to attract love's kiss." Kiss the stone before placing it in the bowl. Then recite the final lines and sprinkle the rose petals over the quartz. Lift the bowl and place it on a windowsill in your house. Leave it there for seven days. On the eighth day, empty the bowl and bury the stone and rose petals at your front door to ensure love finds its way to you.

TO FIND FOREIGN LOVE
ANASTASIA GREYWOLF

True love may come from near or far, and sometimes a foreign love is just what you need to see life anew. To invite a distant lover into your life, perform this spell.

Write your name on a piece of white paper, with blue ink. Roll it up and tie it with a red ribbon. Place it in a red sachet with a sprig of rosemary and a piece of silver. Place a rock from the shore or your home in the sachet as well. Then throw it into the sea.

DATING AND FINDING LOVE

TO UNDERSTAND A FOREIGN LOVER'S LANGUAGE
GRETA GOLDBART

Love may transcend language, but if you want help mastering the same tongue as your foreign love, try this spell.

Language is not only about the tongue, but also involves facial expressions and gestures. For that reason, it is important to pay attention to all of these when casting this spell! First, take a peppermint, and dissolve it in your mouth. Once it is gone and your mouth is fresh, speak the phrase *I speak* in your chosen language. Next, rub your hands with mint-scented lotion and speak the phrase *I feel* in your chosen language. Lastly, rub your face with mint-scented lotion (appropriate for your face) and speak the phrase *I understand* in your chosen language. Learning shall come swiftly to you.

LOVE TEA
JILL ROBI

Take three rose quartz stones (for the mind, the heart, and the spirit) and rub them between your palms over a pot of spring water, blessing it with your intention. Meditate on the type of love you want. Bring the now blessed water to a boil. In an empty mug, add:

1 orange pekoe tea bag
2 tablespoons organic milk
1 tablespoon pure honey
3 drops vanilla
a fresh ginger slice
½ teaspoon ground cinnamon

Take the rose quartz stones and place them on different points of the cup. Pour the boiled water into the mug, focusing again on the love that you want. Let the tea steep for three to five minutes. Pick up the stones and keep them in one hand, and drink the tea slowly with the other.

TO GET SOMEONE TO DREAM ABOUT YOU
LUNA ETERNAL

For this spell, you will need:

   Lavender oil

   1 golden bowl

   Poppy seeds

   1 needle

   2 white candles

   The subjects's hair (if it can be obtained)
      or two pictures of the person.

In the light of a full moon or on a clear night with no clouds, pour the lavender oil in the bowl. Sprinkle in the poppy seeds. Using the needle, carve the name of the person you wish to dream of you close to the top of each side of the candles. Dip your hands into the bowl and rub the oil and poppy seeds on the candles. Light each candle and place one on each side of your bed. Place the hair or pictures under the candles and let them burn until they have erased the person's name. (You will need to have a safe space for them; you do not want anything to catch on fire.) Before you go to sleep, recite this spell while holding the person's hair or pictures:

*This man or woman I want to see
deep in dreams I long to be
Make them see me through the night
to see me in a bright new light
across the earth or waters bound
to find them in their slumbering grounds
dreams to last throughout the night
until awakened by sun's first light*

TO MAKE SOMEONE CONTACT YOU
CALYX REED

This charm will inspire your heart's desire to get into contact with you. If you know someone you like but who could like you a little more, whisper this to yourself before any expected encounter:

*You know you want them,
you know you do.
But somehow they don't contact you.
You see them pass down hallways wide
but fate has not been on your side.
So say this spell: Repeat it twice.
You're bound to find you're what they like.
A drop of good intentions pure,*

A heart that is completely sure.
Three smiles and a friendly nod,
Your smooth approach your friends will laud.
If you are kind and good and true,
then true good love will follow you.
Shoulders back, a friendly smile,
A willingness to talk awhile.
Take it slow and they'll go fast.
A date, a night, your hand they'll ask.
With confidence and manners kind
soon you can say that they are mine.

TO MAKE SOMEONE HAVE LOVING FEELINGS
TRADITIONAL

To move someone to love, her lover must take a blade of grass in his mouth, and turning to the east and the west, say:

Where the sun goes up
Shall my love be by me
Where the sun goes down
There by her I'll be.

Then the blade of grass should be cut up into pieces and mingled with some food, which the girl must eat, and if she swallows the least bit of the grass, she will be *gewogen und treugesinnt*—moved to love and true-hearted.

TO FIND A MATE WITH GOOD QUALITIES
JILL ROBI

On a lavender sheet of paper, write down all of the qualities that you want in a mate. Hold the paper over sage smoke, then fold it eight times, wrapping a ribbon the shade of lavender around it. Place it in your purse, bag, or pocket, so that it's with you at all times.

EYE CONTACT SPELL
ANASTASIA GREYWOLF

To get someone to look at you, even across a crowded room, find a tiger eye (stone) and place it in your pocket. Rub your finger over the stone and stare at the person's third eye—the spot in between their two visible eyes at the top of their nose in their forehead. Focus on placing a question into their mind. Something like "Who is that?" or "Is that (your name)?" work well. If it's meant to be, they will look at you and have an immediate attraction. If not, then it's a sign that if you do get together, things might not be too passionate in the bedroom.

TO GET SOMEONE YOU WORK WITH TO NOTICE YOU
GRETA GOLDBART

A digital spell for the modern mystic! You will need a computer with internet access and an email account.

This spell takes into account the digital nature of many workplaces. First, send an email to yourself with the name of the person you want to notice you as the only text in the body of the email. Once you have received this email from yourself, forward it again to yourself with the addition of your name. Finally, forward it one more time with the addition of the name of your workplace. Once this has been received, delete the email. From then on, watch carefully as the person will begin to notice you more and more.

TO FIND A PURE COMPANION
ELISIA G

You're done with the bad dates, the ones who are like a fast-food fix: greasy and satisfying in the moment, but so regrettable afterwards. You're ready for your good man or woman, the one who comes to you with a heart like a lotus flower and lily-pure hands. Where will find you such a unicorn mate?

The answer, dear one, lies within. In order to find love as radiant as the sun, you're going to have to look in the mirror. You're going to need to prep yourself, because once this person shows up, it's goodbye to all that chaos, hello to the rainbow road.

Start with a bath, or if you've got roommates, swap it for a footbath in the privacy of your boudoir. Fill it with essential oils, rose petals, whatever other pretty things or smells tickle your fancy. Luxuriate in these waters until you feel all the negative energy from your day—or week—leaking out of you, until you have a clear space in your head.

Once you've reached this point (and if you don't reach it, keep repeating the bath ritual until you do), pull out a crystal pendulum. (You can either buy these in magic shops or make one yourself by attaching a crystal to a string, but I recommend buying one, since they are made specifically for clearing energies and can be worn around your neck afterwards to keep protecting and cleansing your space.) Hold the pendulum by the end of its chain and let it hover over your belly button. This is where the astral cord, which connects you to your previous sexual partners, is located. Now, ask your pendulum if it's ready to clear out the energy of these partners. It should start swinging wildly on its own, an enthusiastic "yes." Maintain focus on your swinging crystal, and allow it to whirl around your naval area. The pendulum will swing in wider and wider arcs, cutting the cord between you and your previous partners, disengaging your energy from theirs. Take deep breaths and remain calm while the crystal does its job. Once you feel that all the energy is cleared, put the crystal pendulum around your neck and wear it for a week. It will continue to clear out the emotional debris.

Having a pure slate signals to the universe that you're ready to meet someone cut of the same cloth as yourself. In order to strengthen this law of attraction, do something loving for yourself several times during that week. Buy yourself flowers, give yourself a compliment for a job well done, take yourself out on a date.

The only catch is that you may find that the pure companion you're seeking is yourself. It's also likely you may attract unclean energies during this time due to your squeaky clean, bright nature. Don't fall into that trap! Your pure companion will manifest after this week is up, knowing intuitively to show up at the spell's completion and not while it is in progress.

Tarot cards for your altar: Tower reversed, Two of Cups reversed. The Star, Knight of Cups.

TO FIND "THE ONE"
JILL ROBI

Write one paragraph about your "one." Include the person's hair color, eye color, height, what they do, what they like, etc. Once completed, before you go to sleep, envision this person, then focus on their location. Don't ignore your intuition, for sometimes you may have to go find them (that is, they may not be in your neck of the woods).

FOR FINDING SPRING LOVE
JILL ROBI

On the first day of spring, sit in a meditative position in a patch of sunlight and chant: *New season, new bloom, new love.*

TO FIND LOVE IN THE SUMMER
JAMES BENJAMIN KENYON

How beautiful the summer morn,
With billowy leagues of wheat and corn!
The shining woods and fields rejoice;
Each twinkling stream lifts up its voice
To join the chorus of the sky;

DATING AND FINDING LOVE

O beautiful unspeakably!
In the dry cicada's notes,
In the thistle-down that floats
Aimless on the shimmering air,
In the perfume sweet and rare
Of the sun-steeped, dark-leaved trees,
Dwell the year's deep prophecies.
Hark! the clangor of the mills

Echoes from the drowsy hills.
The foamy clouds, the smiling dale.
The dimpling waves, the laughing flowers,
The low, faint droning of the bees.
Mixed with sweet twitterings from the leas,
Conspire to charm the magic hours.
Under a spell the spirit lies;
Sundered is sorrow's misty veil;
Today life is a glad surprise,
A tranquil rapture, fine and frail.
Wherein to joy-anointed eyes
The old earth seems a Paradise.

TO FIND AUTUMN LOVE
DY EDWARDS

When the days are empty and golden,
And the wind has almost remembered what winter is,
To find what you want—look, quest, seek,
But to find what you need—hold. Still. Breathe.

Love spells are fickle at the best of times,
Because love has its own magic separate from us
    (but part of us),
And those kinds of magic don't always play well
    with others,
I could tell you to be careful, to be safe, but . . . but . . .

DATING AND FINDING LOVE

Love is never safe to start,
There is no way to give or receive it without,
Some element of risk,
Some raising of apple-scented wind,
That at any moment might turn into
    driving painful rain.

For the best way to instill love in another,
Look within and first find what you can give,
And make sure (this is the hard part)
    that you have love for yourself,
Without this you will never know,
When someone wants to give anything to
    the best and worst of you.

To bring love when the days turn gold,
Wear orange and red (scarves and sweaters are best),
And while, yes, pumpkin spice is in everything nice,
If you seek love—apple is better!

Find an orchard that still smells of oversweet apples,
And just-as-sweet honey,
Drink it in, and the dying green smell of the trees,
The red and yellow and green of the fruit,
If you want to (and if you are ready, you probably will).
Smile. Help a stranger get something just out of reach,
Generosity will be repaid in time.
If they sell cider, buy it while the smell
    of the trees is still in the air,

When you are home, mull the drink,
Add clove for warmth,
Cinnamon for luck,
And nutmeg to draw them in,
Sip slowly and feel the heat in your belly,
Sleep early that night as the wind howls,
It remembers what winter is.

The next sunrise,
Open your eyes, twice if you have to,
Record the dreams you had—
They may give directions,
That are not totally clear at the time,
At this point, keep on,
Smile when you want to,
Laugh whenever you can,
Beauty is yours, joy is yours—
And when you have these,
New love will come too.

TO FIND LOVE IN WINTER
SAVANA LEE

From the dormant frozen Earth comes a fire in the heart and a deep longing in the soul. Here is a spell to awaken the blaze of passionate love even in the depth and chill of winter.

DATING AND FINDING LOVE

You will need a sage stick or Palo Santo for smudging, a white or red candle (both if you prefer), a small bundle of fresh pine needles, 1 tablespoon salt for wisdom, ½ cup honey for sweetness and a binding element, and small bowl of snow if your winter graces you with it. (Set it out by the light of the moon and then bring inside to melt in your cauldron or a bowl that has been smudged. If you do not have snow, melt ice made from purified water.) You will also need a wooden spoon and an altar space or tray to set your spell ingredients on.

Light your sage stick from your candles, smudging your body and all ingredients from the left to right. Place the pine needles in the water and stir. Add in salt and honey and mix three times clockwise. Recite the following words:

> *Tempered by the coolness of the Earth and the purity*
> *of the Snow, I call a love to heat the darkest nights.*
> *Transformed from the icy chill, I light flames of desire,*
> *passion, and belonging. Bring me a love with the*
> *wisdom of the Earth and a nature sweet as honey.*

Picture in your mind the qualities of the lover, or even soulmate, you are seeking, such as steadfastness, loyalty, strength, attractiveness, and sense of humor. Do not limit yourself only to physical attributes; let yourself imagine the feelings your love will awaken within you. Place your hands over the bowl palms down, and seal the spell with these words:

LOVE MAGIC

I manifest and awaken from the sleeping Earth a love to warm these winter months, to make them feel as bright as spring and passionate as summer. Bring to me the love of my highest good and desires. So mote it be.

Thank the elements and seasons and declare your ritual circle closed. Pour your mixture outside onto the Earth and let it sink in, bringing your love to life from the beauty of nature.

TO BE ASKED ON A DATE
SUZANNE LAREAU

Sometimes love needs a little push, and that's what this spell does, sweetening your spirit and drawing that new person toward you. Using an edible marker, write on a small, heart-shaped sugar cookie the name of the person you want to ask you out. If there is no specific person you are targeting, you can just write "Love" on the cookie. Tie a red ribbon around a jar of honey, then immerse the cookie deep in the honey (don't worry if it crumbles a bit). Focus your intention, then state it aloud. For example, you could say, "I want X to notice how funny and smart I am, and I want them to ask to spend time with me." Eat a spoonful of the honey. Leave the cookie suspended in the honey until your wish comes true.

FIRST DATE SPELL
JAMES BENJAMIN KENYON

To have success on a first date, find a quiet space to reflect and recite:

> *Ah, what awaits us when the glimmering sight*
> *Is slowly quenched within the gathering night;*
> *When on the hills the purple shadows fall,*
> *And lingering darkness hides and covers all—*
> *New life, new love?*
>
> *Than is the old could new life sweeter be?*
> *Than now hath love some rarer ecstacy?*
> *Ah, while the day shines, and it grows not late,*
> *Say not there dwell beyond the night's dark gate*
> *New life, new love.*

FIRST DATE CHARM
GEMMA ARONSON

First dates can be nerve-racking, but this spell will calm your nerves and help you seem more attractive and interesting to your date.

You will need rainwater, rose petals, a stick of cinnamon, a white or buff cloth, cotton string or natural twine, and natural quartz.

Bring your rainwater to boil in a small pan. Gently place the rose petals on top of the water. With your cinnamon stick, stir the petals into the water in a clockwise motion seven times. Leave the cinnamon and petals in the water until it cools to body temperature.

Lay out your cloth and place your crystal in the center. Remove the cinnamon stick from the water and use it to rub the infused water into the insides of your wrists and the bottom of your throat. Place the cinnamon next to the crystal and chant:

> *Grant me beauty, splendor, and calm*
> *With these petals I will charm*

Now say your date's full name twice.

Pull the four corners of the cloth together with the crystal and cinnamon inside to form a small charm pouch. Tie the pouch together with the string by winding it around twice. Tie it with two knots.

Place the charm pouch in your bag and keep it with you on your date.

PERFUME CHARM FOR A FIRST DATE
GRETA GOLDBART

This simple perfume will bring you good energy on a date.

Mix 2 tablespoons of coconut oil with four drops each of ylang-ylang, tuberose, and bergamot essential oils. Wear this mixture on your pulse points (wrist, throat, sternum area) when you go on your date.

SPELL FOR A BLIND DATE
GRETA GOLDBART

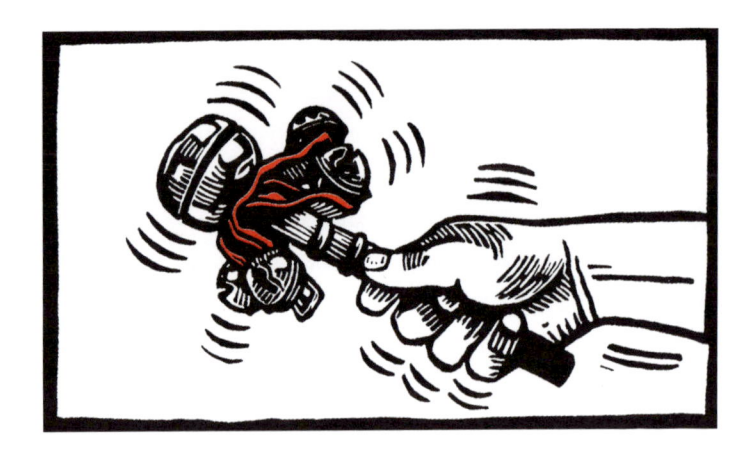

For this spell, you will need three white votive candles, vetiver oil, a toothpick, and a small bell.

On the evening of your blind date, place your candles in a row and light them. Let them burn until there is a pool of wax surrounding the wick. Place three to five drops of vetiver oil in each candle, stirring gently with a toothpick. Recite this incantation facing the candles, ringing your bell between each line:

> *I know not whom I shall meet* (Ring bell)
> *I know not how I shall seem* (Ring bell)
> *Let fate decide tonight* (Ring bell)
> *If this romance is wrong or right.* (Ring bell)

Blow out the candles and go on your date.

GOOD DATE CHARM
JILL ROBI

On a piece of rose-colored paper, write a list of the elements you feel make a good date, such as time, place, activity, outfit (yours and your date's). Fold it and place it in a white sachet with mint and juniper berries. Sleep with the sachet the night before your date, and carry it with you until your date is over.

TO BE ASKED TO THE PROM OR A DANCE
JILL ROBI

On a Sunday night, anoint a rose-colored pillar candle with vanilla and almond oil. In a quiet, dark space, light the candle, mentally drawing the positive energy into yourself. With your eyes closed chant: *I invite you to invite me*. Repeat this spell every Sunday night for a month.

TO BE ASKED TO A SPECIAL EVENT
JILL ROBI

In a red satchel, place red sardonyx, rosemary, and sage. On the night of a full moon, in a patch of moonlight, meditate with the satchel, then chant, *Doors will open and invitations will come.*

TO CALM NERVES BEFORE A DATE
SUZANNE LAREAU

It's natural to be a bit anxious before meeting a new person, and those jitters can be especially intense if you are hoping for a romantic connection. Before a date, soothe your nerves with the following ritual designed to dispel negative energy, promote peace, and ensure that you are attractive to your potential mate. Plus, it will make you smell lovely, which never hurts.

First, make purple witches' salt: grind with a mortar and pestle 2 tablespoons sea salt together with 1 tablespoon dried lavender and lilac (you can use only lavender, if you prefer). Be sure that, as you grind the mixture, the crushed flowers release their fragrant oils into the salt, perfuming the mix. Lavender signifies love, peace, and protection while lilac brings wisdom, memory, and good luck.

Several hours before your date, drape a pink silk or cotton scarf around the frame of your bathroom mirror (or the mirror you will use as you get ready to go out) to encourage a positive self-image. Pink is a color of the heart and is associated with romance and tenderness. (The passion of red can come later!)

Light a small pink candle in your bathroom and draw a bath. Focus your intention as you sprinkle a small amount of the purple witches' salt into your bathwater. Remember the truism that "salt does what you tell it to"—so keep your thoughts positive. Anticipate with pleasure the wonderful time you will have on your date as you get to know this new person who may one day be very special to you. Bathe in the blessed water, breathing deeply and evenly as you prepare for your evening out.

Get ready for your date in front of the pink-draped mirror, continuing to focus your intention for the date and breathing slowly and deeply. Listening to your favorite music can help discharge some nerves and prevent the preparation from feeling too intense—think light and fun. If possible, allow the candle to burn down naturally as you prepare for your date. Then, go out and have a good time!

FOR GOOD LUCK ON A DATING APP
GABRIEL GREY

To have luck finding a good match on a dating app, write the qualities you want in a mate or relationship on a label or piece of tape, then place it on the back of your phone. Don't let anyone see the list. (If you have a phone case, place it between your phone and the case.) Sit on a red couch, chair, cushion, or blanket as you use the app. It will lead good mates who are full of the qualities you desire to find you.

FOR GOOD LUCK ON A DATE
JILL ROBI

Inside a sachet, place a sprig of lavender, rose petals, and a mixture of the following natural stones: moonstone, hematite, citrine, rose quartz, and sun stone. Meditate with the sachet, bringing forth your inner brilliance. Chant, *I invite love into my life*. A dark room with a few tea candles is best suited for this purpose. Once complete, carry out your typical dating rituals. Take the sachet with you for positive energy and to make you irresistibly intriguing to your date.

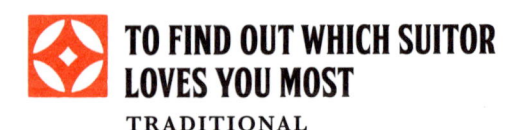

TO FIND OUT WHICH SUITOR LOVES YOU MOST
TRADITIONAL

If you have multiple suitors and you want to know which loves you more deeply, get some chestnuts and write the initials of each suitor on them. Line up the chestnuts on a grate above a fire. The nut that moves first will show you the one who loves you most.

TO FIND OUT IF YOUR DATE IS AFRAID OF COMMITMENT
GRETA GOLDBART

You will need a small, smooth rock, a black marker or paint, and an outfit with pockets.

On one side of the smooth rock, write YES and on the other write NO. Before you leave for your date, hold the stone in your cupped hands and ask: *Should I beware my lover's flight?*

Keep the stone in your pocket. Turn it over in your pocket each time your date says your name. When you get home, pull the stone out—your question will be answered.

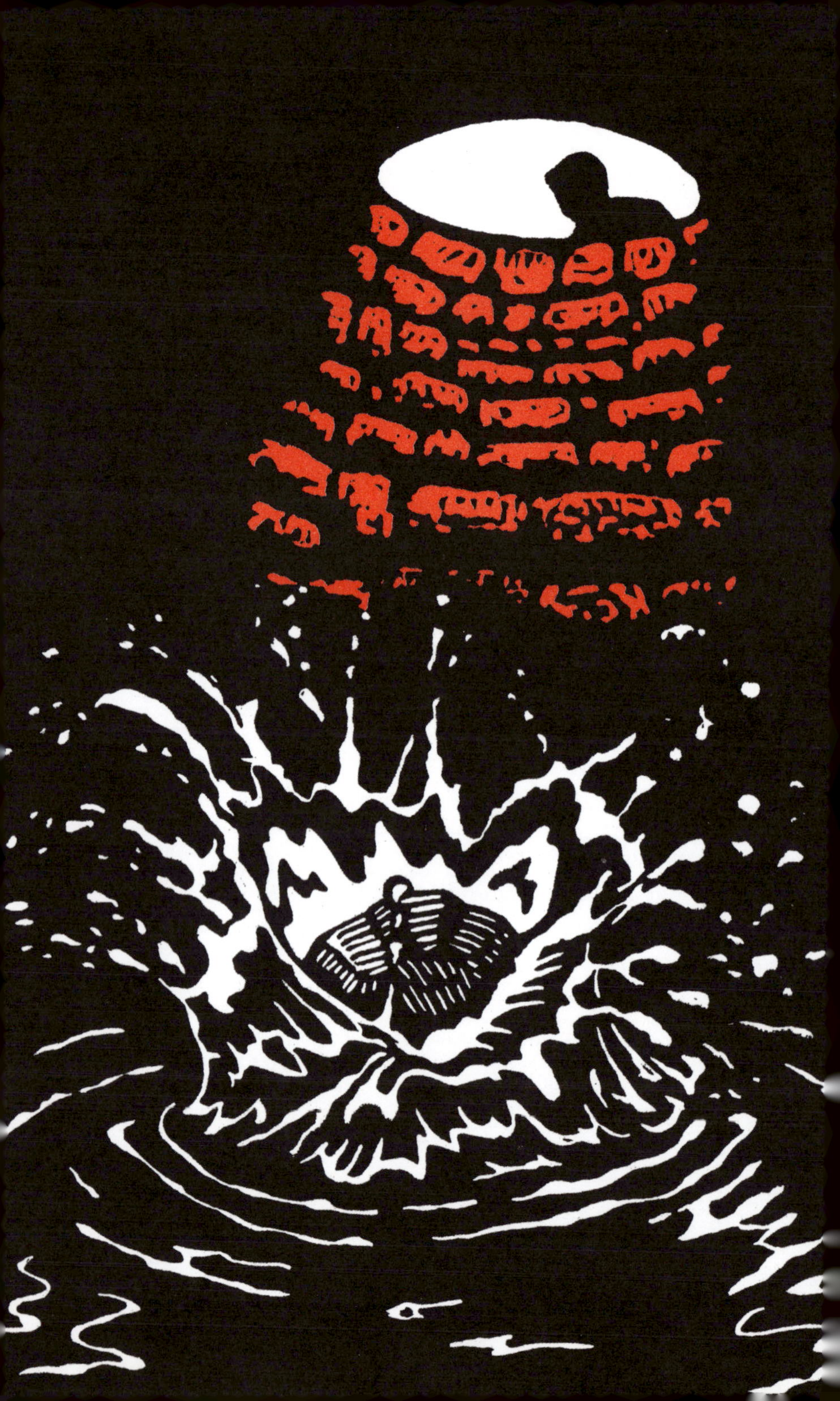

SPELLS TO SEE YOUR LOVE LIFE'S FUTURE

TO KNOW HOW MANY LOVERS YOU WILL HAVE
ANASTASIA GREYWOLF

To know how many lovers you'll have, recite the following spell before going to sleep:

> *I don't need a spouse to know I'm great*
> *And I'm not interested in a steady mate*
> *What I want to know is what my loins suggest:*
> *At the end of my life, who will attest?*
> *Who will know me in a way that makes them blush?*
> *Who will say my name only in a hush?*
> *And who will remember me with a never-ending lifelong crush?*
> *Tell me how many I'll light on fire*
> *And I swear to Aphrodite I'll fulfill their desire.*

The numbers of hours you sleep that night is the number of true lovers you will have. (If you sleep longer than twelve hours, you will have some number more than twelve). Many also report dreaming of future lovers while they sleep!

MIRROR CHARM TO SEE YOUR LOVE
TRADITIONAL

The night before a full moon, take a hand mirror (preferably one that is antique, especially a family heirloom) and hold it in front of your face. Close your eyes and walk backwards toward your bed, repeating: *Come to me, come to me, come to me.* When you fall upon your bed, open your eyes and look into the mirror. You may catch a glimpse of the person you'll marry rushing over to help you.

TO FIND OUT WHOM YOU'LL END UP WITH
TRADITIONAL

If you wish to know whom you will wed, buy a ring; it doesn't need to be gold, so long as it has the semblance of a wedding ring; and it is best to try this charm on your own birthday. Pay for your ring with cash, and give the change you receive to the first person who asks for it in the street. If no one asks, you must give it to someone less fortunate than you. Carefully note what they say in return. When you get home, write what was said down on a sheet of paper at each of the four corners, and, in the middle, put the two first letters of your name, your age, and your astrological sign.

Get a branch of olive and fasten the ring on the stalk with a string of thread that has been steeped all day in a mixture of honey and vinegar (or any composition of opposite qualities, such as very sweet and very sour). Cover your ring and stalk with the written paper, carefully wrapping round and round. Put it in your pocket or wear the ring around your neck; visit a graveyard at nine o'clock at night and bury the charm in the grave of a young man who died unmarried; and, while you are so doing, repeat the letters of your name three times backwards.

Return home, and keep as silent as possible until you go to bed, which must be done before eleven; put a light in your chimney, or some safe place; and, before midnight, or just about that time, a vision of your future spouse will present itself at the foot of the bed, but will presently disappear. If you are not to marry, none will come. However, your future children or future lovers may visit the foot of your bed instead.

FOR SEEING THE FUTURE OF YOUR MARRIAGE
TRADITIONAL

To see the future of your marriage, perform the following spell on the third night of a new moon. You will need:

- 1 teaspoon brandy
- 1 teaspoon rum
- 1 teaspoon gin
- 1 teaspoon wine
- 1 teaspoon olive oil
- 1 tablespoon cream
- 3 tablespoons spring water

SPELLS TO SEE YOUR LOVE LIFE'S FUTURE

Mix the ingredients together and drink it as you get into bed and recite:

> *This mixture of love I take for my potion,*
> *That I of my destiny may have a notion;*
> *Cupid befriend me, new moon be kind,*
> *And show unto me that fate that's designed.*

You will dream of drink, and according to the quality or manner of it being presented, you may tell the condition to which you will rise or fall by marriage. If you dream of water, you will live in poverty; Champagne or spirits, prosperity. If you dream of drinking too much, you will fall, at a future period, into that sad error yourself, without great care. If you dream of a drunken man, it is ominous that you will have a drunken mate. But if you dream of a man drinking coffee, he will be a hard worker.

TO KNOW THE NAME OF THE PERSON ONE IS TO MARRY
TRADITIONAL

Take a stone of rather large size, as round as you can get it, and go by night to a covered well; it is best if it were in the middle of some field or garden. And just as the clock strikes one, cast the stone, *con gran fracasso*—with as much noise as you can make—into the water.

Then listen with care to hear the sound produced by the fall of the stone. Although it may be a little obscure or confused, and not always very intelligible, with a little patience and attention one can detect in the sound that the stone makes in the water the name of the person whom one is to marry.

TO KNOW WHAT COLOR HAIR YOUR LOVER WILL HAVE
ANASTASIA GREYWOLF

To know what color hair your future lover will have, gather a bunch of hair from an animal with a strong spirit. It should be an animal that is unknown and a little

SPELLS TO SEE YOUR LOVE LIFE'S FUTURE

mysterious to you. A warthog has proven results, but a horse may also be used. Dip the bunch of hair into red paint, and say the spell below. Every time you say the name of a hair color, let a drop of paint drip from the hair onto a piece of white paper. When you're done with the spell, see which dot on the paper is biggest. That is the color hair the love of your life will have.

> *Oh tell me, tell me, simple stain*
> *What hue shall be my beloved's mane?*
> *Will it be black, like the night?*
> *Or bright and blond, full of light?*
> *Will it be orange, or closer to red?*
> *Or perhaps he's older, with a gray head?*
> *Maybe he dyes it, any shade he can get.*
> *Or perhaps he's just an average brunette.*
> *Whatever it is, whatever it be,*
> *Send a simple sign for me.*

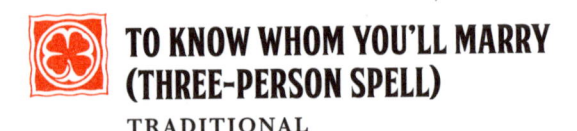

TO KNOW WHOM YOU'LL MARRY (THREE-PERSON SPELL)
TRADITIONAL

To discern whom they shall marry, three young maidens should join together in making a long chain—about a yard will do—of Christmas juniper and mistletoe berries, and, at the end of every link, put an oak acorn. Exactly before midnight let them assemble in a room by themselves, where no one can disturb them; leave a window open, and take the key out of the keyhole and hang it over the chimney-piece; have a good fire. Together, the three maidens should then take a piece of firewood from the pile that is long and thin. Sprinkle it with salt, then wrap the juniper garland around it over and over until it is spent. The women should then sit crosslegged, each with a book in her lap, and read (or pretend to read).

Just as the last acorn is burned, the future husband will cross the room; each one will see her own proper spouse, but he will be invisible to the rest of the wakeful maidens. Those who are not to be wed will see a coffin, or some misshapen form, cross the room. This must be done either on a Wednesday or Friday night, but no other.

TO SEE YOUR FUTURE MATE IN A DREAM
GABRIEL GREY

To see your future mate in a dream, take an egg and roll it all over your body. Then boil it, and slice it in half with the shell still on. Take one half to a place nearby that signifies a crossroads to you. Bury the egg half there.

Go home, and sprinkle sea salt on the remaining egg half. Eat the egg, consuming the white first and the yolk last. Bury the shell near the roots of a plant that has no new shoots. Look for a new shoot each morning. The morning you see a new shoot, recall your dreams from the previous night. The person you saw in your dream will become an important romantic figure in your life.

ASH TREE CHARM
TRADITIONAL

If you come across an ash tree, take a twig from it and place it under your pillow. On the night of the full moon, recite:

Ashen tree, ashen tree
My future love I want to see

You will dream of your future husband or wife.

QUEEN OF CUPS TAROT CHARM
ELISIA G

The Queen of Cups represents a person's connection to their emotional self. She is a great energy to call into your life anytime you need to nurture your dreams or an important relationship—be it with yourself, with others, or for a project. If you're looking to foster creativity, receptivity, or intuition, then she's a guiding presence. Because this queen is frequently depicted holding a cup, the symbol of her emotional center, you can integrate her vision into yours by building your very own Queen of Cups chalise.

This cup does not have to be a cup, strictly speaking. It can be an aquarium, filled with sand and water, with glow-in-the-dark stars floating between ferns and colorful bottles. It can be a magnificent papier-mâché chalice of

SPELLS TO SEE YOUR LOVE LIFE'S FUTURE

magazines and pictures of things you love that you fill to the brim with whatever you're trying to manifest: money, a Leonardo DiCaprio look-alike. Your cup can also be a minimalist invention of white walls and toothpicks painted black, strategically arranged to look like stick figures browsing a museum on holiday. There are no rules on how to build your cup. You also do not need to have an end goal in mind. The most important thing is that the cup represents facets of yourself.

The second piece of magic is to keep your mind focused on your intention as you work. If you're calling on the Queen of Cups because you want to be receptive to the gifts of the universe, then keep your mind relaxed, trusting that your open nature will allow what you need to drop into your lap. If you're calling on her because you want to be more connected to your creative waters, then notice how creative you are being in that moment! If you're searching for clarity on an important issue that needs the heart's voice and not the head—like whether to get engaged or take a new job that looks good on paper but doesn't feel quite right—then use the time you spend constructing your cup to make a space where you aren't trying to puzzle out a logical answer, but are instead diving into your deep, emotional intuitive waters, trusting that the universe will give you a sign to the right direction.

It is said that Tibetan monks create their famous singing bowls while meditating on world peace. Every time one of their bowls is played, it sings out that intention to the universe. By building your own cup, and setting an intention as you build it, it fulfills a similar logic. Make the space to connect to your waters, and once you reconnect to the world outside, the answer or gift that you're seeking will fall right into it.

TO LEARN THE FIRST INITIAL OF ONE'S INTENDED
TRADITIONAL

Pare an apple so that the peel remains in one long piece. Swing this around your head three times and throw it on the floor. The letter it forms will be the initial of your intended sweetheart's name.

TO FIND ANSWERS ABOUT YOUR BELOVED
ANASTASIA GREYWOLF

Make a pendant with garnet or opal and leather string. When there is a new moon, light sage and clear a space by wafting it. Wear the pendant while nearby someone you love for at least seven days. (It doesn't have to be on consecutive days.) If you have a question about your love, hold the pendant over a lit pink or red candle and watch which way it swings. If it swings from left to right in front of you, it means no. If it swings toward and away from you, it means yes.

TO DISCERN IF A LOVE LETTER IS TRUE AND TO KNOW THE FUTURE OF ITS WRITER
TRADITIONAL

On receiving a love letter that has any particular declaration in it, lay it wide open; then fold it in nine folds; pin it next to your heart; and thus wear it till bedtime. Then lay it under your pillow as you sleep. If you dream of gold, diamonds, or any other costly gem, your lover is true, and means what he says; if you dream of white linen, washing, or graves you will lose him by death; and if of flowers he will prove false. If you dream of his saluting you, he means not what he professes and will draw you into a snare. If you dream of castles or a clear sky, there is no deceit, and you will prosper; trees in blossom denote children; and water shows that your lover is faithful, but that you will go through severe poverty for some time, though all may end well.

TO SEE YOUR LOVER'S FLAWS
JILL ROBI

Make rosewater by taking the petals of a red rose and placing them in a pot of distilled water. Over medium-low heat, bring the water to a simmer, and then turn it off and let it steep for one hour. Once done, put some into a clean, clear glass.

Take a photo of your lover, and coat it in the remaining rosewater.

Line a clay bowl in red rose petals, then place the soaked photo inside of it. If it is safe for you to do so, take a small amount of lighter fluid, and put a few drops on each corner, side, and middle of the photo. Drop a match into it, setting the photo aflame. Chant "reveal" as the flames dance across the photo, then pour the remaining rosewater on top. Holding the bowl, continue to chant "reveal" as you keep your eyes closed for ninety seconds or so, focusing on your lover in your mind's eye, seeing their true nature.

TO KNOW IF YOU SHOULD BREAK UP
ANASTASIA GREYWOLF

On a white piece of paper with black ink, ask if you should break up with your partner, or pose another specific question that would allow you to know if the relationship should end. Burn the paper with the flame of a black candle and say: *I release this question to you* ["the world" or a name of a god or goddess who speaks to you] *and await your reply.*

Go to sleep and when you awake, write down everything in your mind. Eat sage with your breakfast or steep some in tea and drink it. Go back to what you wrote and it will help you know your answer.

TO SEE YOUR NEXT LOVER
TRADITIONAL

To see a vision of your next love in a dream, take a sprig of rosemary and a sprig of thyme and place one in each shoe. Place the shoes in a "T" shape at the foot of your bed. Go to sleep and you'll see your future lover in a dream.

MULE LOVE CHARM
TRADITIONAL

If you come across a mule, you can use him to find out if you'll find love soon. Whisper into his ear, "Will my love come soon?" If the mules shakes his head, the answer is yes. If he doesn't move, the answer is no. If he twitches one ear only, the answer is maybe.

SPELLS TO SEE YOUR LOVE LIFE'S FUTURE

TO KNOW IF A MATE IS UNTRUE
SUZANNE LAREAU

If you suspect that your beloved's attention is fixed on another person, perform this spell to see if they are true. Purchase or make a small personal gift for your mate. For best results, choose a present that has deep meaning for you and your partner, for example, a framed menu from the restaurant where you had your first date or a keychain stamped with your pet name for your love.

Braid together three strands of ribbon or embroidery thread in colors of aqua (which promotes communication and growing awareness), white (representing truth), and red (denoting love and passion). Wrap the gift in white tissue paper and bind the package with the braided strand, securing it with a knot. As you tie the knot, focus your thoughts on your question about your mate's fidelity and repeat three times: *May the truth I seek be shown to me.*

If your lover breaks or cuts the strands or unties the knot to free the gift, they are unfaithful. If, however, your mate preserves the knot when opening the package, your bond is strong and your beloved is true. Keep in mind that this spell offers a glimpse into the inner workings of the heart; it is possible that your lover has strayed in thought but not (yet) in deed.

TO KNOW IF A LOVE IS OVER
ALICE CORBIN

Find a rock that has been worn smooth by water and place it under your pillow. Hold it each day and recite:

> *Love me at last, or if you will not,*
> *Leave me;*
> *Hard words could never, as these half-words,*
> *Grieve me:*
> *Love me at last—or leave me.*
>
> *Love me at last, or let the last word uttered*
> *Be but your own;*
> *Love me, or leave me—as a cloud, a vapor,*
> *Or a bird flown.*
> *Love me at last—I am but sliding water*
> *Over a stone.*

Every day, you will feel your love either move further from you or closer, and after twelve days you will know your answer.

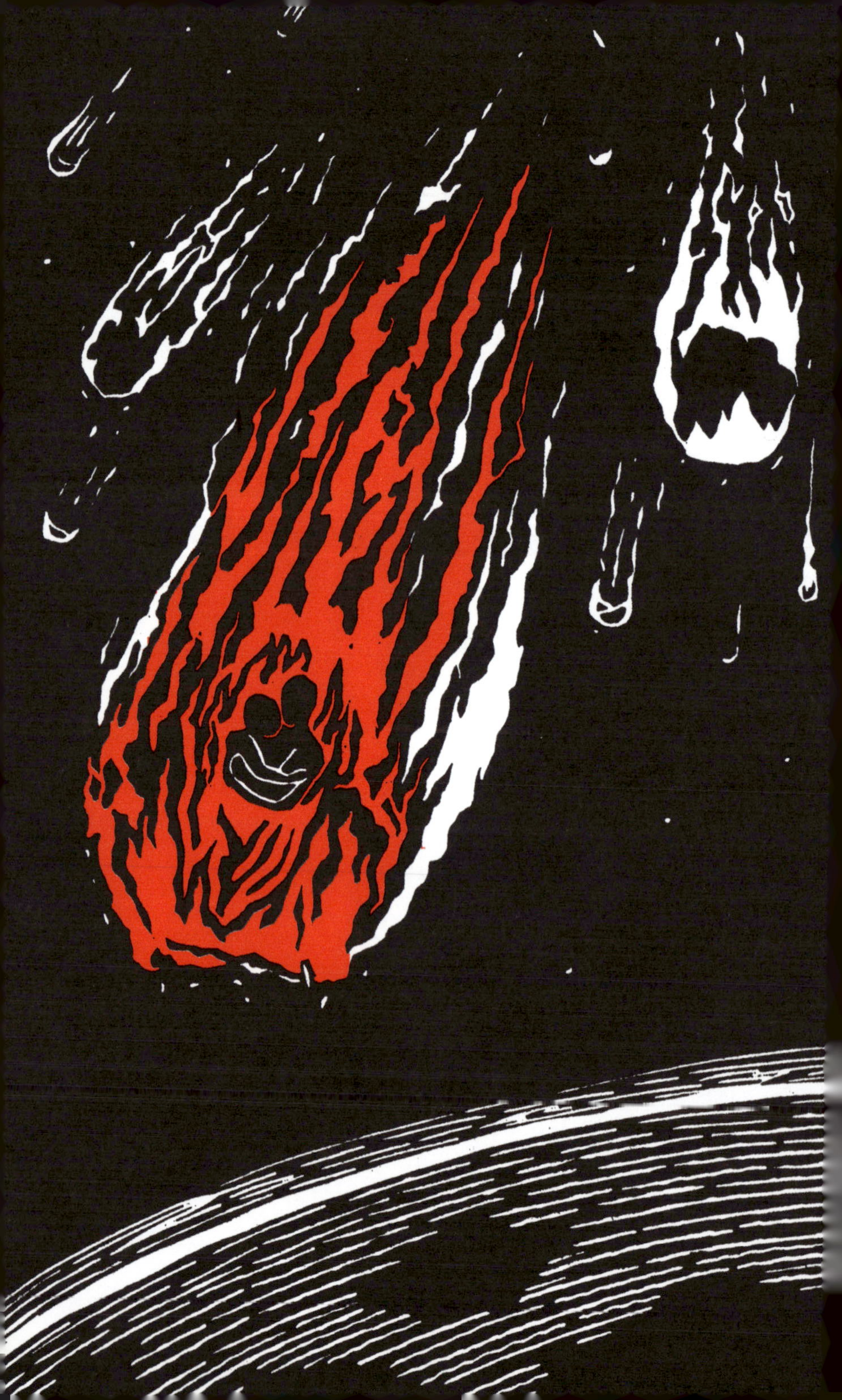

PASSION AND ROMANCE SPELLS

POTION FOR YOUR MOST PASSIONATE AND HIGHEST SELF
SAVANA LEE

Awaken your passion for your most infinite self with this potion. You will need:

- ⅓ cup fresh lavender
- 1 teaspoon cinnamon
- 1 teaspoon licorice root
- 1 cup Dead Sea salt
- Rose petals
- 1 cup raw honey

For the rose petals, choose a color or colors that call to you (pick the first ones you are drawn to). Mix all the dry ingredients in your cauldron or a white bowl that has been smudged. Set out the bowl by the light of the New Moon to absorb the energies of new beginnings and revelations. Add honey when ready to use and then pour into hot water for bathing or steam for your face. Light a black candle. Inhale and recite:

> *I reveal my true self. I am awakened to my true nature. I am surrounded by all my light, love, and the highest good. I claim my power and my passion. I accept all parts of me created from sun and shadow. I am whole.*

Let the fire of your true nature arise. Cherish your individual strength and passions. Let them wash over you until your inner goddess is awakened. Repeat as needed to reabsorb your true nature and find your infinite potential.

PASSION COCKTAIL
JENNIFER BOUDINOT

To bring about passion between yourself and someone else, drink this cocktail together. You'll need:

- 5 ounces gin
- 1 lemon that has been touched by the object of your desire
- 2 ounces simple syrup (sugar dissolved in water)
- 2 ounces elderflower liqueur
- 5 dashes orange bitters
- 8–10 basil leaves

Begin by taking the gin and dipping a bit of your skin (preferably an erogenous zone) into it. Combine the gin with the juice of the lemon that the other person has touched, the simple syrup, the elderflower liqueur, and the orange bitters. Take a bunch of basil and crush the leaves between two garnets, rose quartz, or stones that have meaning to you or the other person. Shake the smashed leaves with the rest of the ingredients and ice. While you're shaking, think loving thoughts about yourself and the other person. Pour the concoction into two separate glasses and drink with the object of your desire. Just make sure not to drink too much!

PASSION POTION
JILL ROBI

Take carnelian stones, enough to cover the bottom of a glass. Pour spring water over them, filling the glass to the top. With both hands on the glass, focus your energy and chant, *Break all negative ties, and may my passions arise*, for several minutes. Let the water sit at room temperature for seven hours. Once it's had time to properly infuse, remove the stones and say the incantation before drinking it, and once more after.

INCANTATION BEFORE WRITING A LOVE LETTER
JEANNE DE LA WARE

Face to the south—the direction associated with the element of fire and the spark of inspiration. Light a pure white candle, center it in front of your writing paper, and recite:

> *I put ink to paper to my beloved, ensured*
> *of my adoration, sparked by [his/her/their] allure.*
> *For clear thoughts while writing, my candle is white,*

For passion inspired, red is its light.
I call upon cardamom, spicy and sweet,
to help me entice my beloved-to-be.
Sapphire, the gift between faithful lovers,
don't let my beloved fall for another.
I invoke gold and iron, forged in fire,
to strengthen my bond with my heart's desire.

INCANTATION BEFORE WRITING A TEXT MESSAGE OR E-MAIL
JILL ROBI

Take an undyed feather, preferably goose or duck, and hold it on top of your phone. Sitting down in a quiet, dark area, chant, *Let the right words flow through me. Let the right words reach [person's name]*. After several minutes, and once your breathing has been regulated, compose your message.

TO BRING ABOUT PASSIONATE MEMORIES
GEMMA ARONSON

Do you want your lover to remember a special romantic moment you shared? Or do you want your ex to be reminded of a passionate memory? For this spell, you will need:

- 1 white candle
- Rose oil
- 2 red candles
- Photo of your lover or ex
- Metal dish or chalice

This memory spell will ignite passion in your relationship or help your ex remember how much love was between you. Perform it under a waxing moon.

Etch your lover's name along the length of the white candle. Anoint the candle with the rose oil, starting at the

PASSION AND ROMANCE SPELLS

middle and working your way to the top of the candle and then down to the bottom.

Place the white candle in between the two red candles and light them.

Close your eyes and get yourself into a meditative state. Relive in your mind's eye the passionate or romantic moment that you want your lover to remember. Then chant:

> *Blessed be the oil of love*
> *Under the beauteous moon above*
> *Recount the passion of thy love*

Hold your lover's photo in your hands and stare into their eyes. Imagine your lover rekindling your memory. Place the photo in the dish or chalice, making sure not to let any of the photo's edges overlap the sides.

Pour molten wax from the white candle onto the photo. It needs to cover the photo completely. Chant your lover's name three times as you do so.

After the candles have burnt down and the wax is no longer hot, remove the wax-covered photo and keep it under your pillow for at least four nights or until the moon starts waning.

TO IGNITE PASSIONATE DREAMS
TRADITIONAL

Take a length of red ribbon and keep it with you all day, touching it as often as possible and thinking about your lover when you do. Then, place the ribbon under your lover's pillow. He or she will have romantic dreams about you and awake full of passion.

LUST CHARM
ANASTASIA GREYWOLF

If you have trouble feeling passion in romantic situations, this charm can help bring it back. You'll need:

    1 peach

    ½ cup sugar

    2 tablespoons avocado oil

    2 teaspoons grated ginger

First, peel and mash the peach. Then mix the pulp with the sugar, avocado oil, and ginger. Rub the mixture all over your body, especially in the erotic zones (although not on any sensitive areas). Leave it on for as long as possible before washing it off. Try to apply as close as possible to the time when you want to feel passion and romance.

CHAMPAGNE LOVE CHARM
ANASTASIA GREYWOLF

You will need two glasses of champagne to which you've added three drops of elderflower liqueur. Chant:

> *May this charm*
> *Ignite our love*
> *On this night*

Drop a strawberry into each glass, share one glass with your love, and drink it together.

TO MAKE YOURSELF ATTRACTED TO SOMEONE YOU LOVE
JILL ROBI

On an unmarred piece of lavender paper, write the individual characteristics that you find attractive in a mate, such as hands, lips, broad shoulders, etc. Below this list, write the individual characteristics that you find attractive in the person you love. Burn the petals of a rose with sage, then fold the paper and place it on top. Take the ashes and put them in a sachet while chanting, *Odylic force*. Place the sachet inside your pillowcase.

"NEXT LEVEL" PASSION CHARM
GABRIEL GREY

Use this charm if there's someone you are hoping to get physical with. Melt the following in a mason jar submerged a saucepan of warm water:

- 2 tablespoons beeswax pellets
- 1 teaspoon avocado oil
- 1 strand of your beloved's hair
- 1 dried mushroom (chopped)
- 1 germ of wheat
- 1 rose petal
- Dash vanilla extract

Mix this combination while heating over medium flame, then pour into a heart-shaped mold or ice cube tray. Before an occasion where you will see this person, rub a heart over your heart and on your face. If the person doesn't initiate something, then it wasn't meant to be.

TO REAWAKEN PASSION
SUSAN ADCOX

Those who have a steadfast partner are indeed lucky, but sometimes we need an ardent lover as well. This spell is for those times when everyday life has taken precedence over passion. To cast this spell, rely upon the tried and true elements of love spells. A fresh rose and two red candles will serve as powerful amulets for arousing desire. After lighting the candles near the rose, recite:

> *Dewdrops tremble on the rose*
> *In the flame our passion grows.*
> *Let our sweetness be distilled*
> *Until we're swept away, unwilled.*

KISSING CHARM
TRADITIONAL

If there's someone you want to kiss you, write the person's name in blue ink on white paper three times. Then write your name in red ink on top of their name. Fold the paper in half and place it at the bottom of a bowl of honey. Place a dab of the honey on your lips before seeing the person you desire. If they've been wanting to kiss you too, they'll take the opportunity.

BED SPELL
ANASTASIA GREYWOLF

To enchant your bed so that you always have good sex in it, sprinkle rosewater on it. Then sprinkle rose petals on it while reciting:

> *In this bed, I can be me*
> *I am sexy, I am free*
> *There is no blemish*
> *No extra weight*
> *No reason to feel that I'm not the best date*

> *In this bed, I can be me,*
> *I am sexy, I am free*
> *All of my wounds will magically heal*
> *I will enjoy myself and be completely real*

Sprinkle the rosewater on yourself and then roll around in the rose petals until you start to laugh.

BED SACHET
JILL ROBI

Anoint rose petals with coconut oil. Place them in a red sachet with cinnamon and woodruff. Charge the sachet by chanting, *Passion be kind; passion be mine.* Keep this sachet either under your bed or underneath or inside the place (such as a couch or a counter) where you want to make passionate love.

TO MAKE YOUR LOVER DESIRE YOU
GRETA GOLDBART

Invite your lover over for a romantic dinner. Prepare a recipe that you both will enjoy, with one stipulation—it must contain saffron. When you add the saffron, stir the food three times clockwise, once counterclockwise, and again three times clockwise. Serve it to your lover with a garnish of parsley. Complete the meal with vanilla ice cream.

You will find that after the meal your lover will become increasingly attracted to you.

APHRODISIACS TO BRING OUT PASSION
ANASTASIA GREYWOLF

To increase passion in the bedroom, you and your partner simply need to eat the right foods during the day. At breakfast, cut an avocado in half and have your partner eat one half while you eat the other. Eat something spicy for lunch, and add in some artichokes if possible! At midday, have a chai tea if you are looking for something to drink, and eat pumpkin seeds as a snack throughout the day. For dinner, it's best to start off with some oysters, then follow them up with a light pasta with pesto made from scratch with olive oil, basil, and pine nuts. Finish with a tray of dark chocolate and fruit, especially strawberries, cherries, and pomegranate seeds. You'll barely be done eating before you find yourself in the bedroom.

TO REKINDLE PASSION
THOMAS JENKINS

Light four candles, and place them at the four corners of the bed you share with your lover. Set an article of clothing belonging to each of the intended recipients of the spell on the bed. Speak aloud at the foot of the bed:

> *May old joys be reclaimed and new ones created. May these lovers view each other with fresh eyes and earned love, and may the passion that has waned once again burn brightly.*
>
> *I declare this bed a sanctum, where the rages of life fall to the tender calm of compassion, where the bonds of love form a bulwark against fear, anger, jealousy, and spite, and where passion is expressed freely and without shame or reservation.*

Kiss each pillow on the bed. Allow the candles to burn down.

NEW IDEAS IN BED SPELL
THOMAS JENKINS

We often seek new experiences with our sexual partners. This spell will bless and encourage such activities. It can be performed with your partner(s) before experiencing something new or alone before approaching your partner about a fantasy.

Write down the activity you wish to try with your partner. Boil a pot of water. Steep rosehip tea in the water, adding to the mixture the slip of paper on which you have written your desire. Recite:

> *We share our bodies and minds, joining together in passion. May we expose our true selves, rendering ourselves truly naked to each other. We shall seek joy and pleasure shamelessly, and without reservation. We will be each other's desire, and use our connection to grow, doubling our love and our joy, opening the secret caves in our hearts and joining together without judgment. Fear has no place in our bond and shall be replaced with trust.*

Remove the slip of paper from the tea. Share the tea with your partner.

HIDE YOUR FLAWS FROM YOUR LOVER
GEMMA ARONSON

This spell is for anyone who wants hide their flaws from a lover or potential lover.

Gather one walnut for each flaw you want to hide, paper, and a pencil.

PASSION AND ROMANCE SPELLS

Place a red candle and a gold candle in front of you and light them. Close your eyes and concentrate on the first flaw that you want to conceal. Open the walnut shell, remove the nut, and eat it.

Write out the flaw you wish to conceal on a small piece of paper. Be sure to write your flaw as "I am not" rather than "I am." For example, if your flaw is jealousy, write: "I am not a jealous person."

Fold the paper and place it inside the shell where the nut was. Repeat, using a new walnut for each flaw.

Bury the walnut(s) in the ground near a stream or river. As you cover the walnut in soil, chant your lover's name in your mind three times.

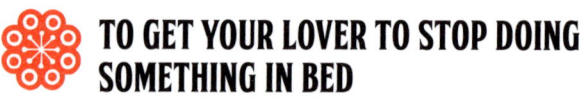

TO GET YOUR LOVER TO STOP DOING SOMETHING IN BED
GRETA GOLDBART

Sometime before going to bed, perhaps in the daytime or early evening, sit by yourself in a quiet space. Light a sandalwood candle or incense, and take a few deep, calming breaths. Picture the action you want to end or change. Visualize it changing into something you would rather happen instead. Continue your calming breathing. Focus on the image of what you want to happen and think this phrase until it feels natural: *What I want is important.* Then, begin to speak the phrase aloud until you feel comfortable saying it. When it feels natural to say it, you have completed the meditation.

When you are about to go to bed, light the same kind of incense or the same candle. Sandalwood is not only an empowering scent, but also an aphrodisiac. Your lover will pick up on your aversion to a particular action and will cease doing it.

Of course, if you find this spell is not working for you, it is important to open the lines of communication with your lover and tell them what you like and do not like!

TO ENHANCE A MATE'S LOVEMAKING
SUSAN ADCOX

When two people come together to please each other, the results can be mundane or out of this world. Use these charms to fire your partner's passion and ensure astral coupling. Incorporate the color red into your ritual by lighting a crimson candle, spreading rose petals, or putting on a red garment before repeating the spell. Patchouli oil may enhance erotic energy, but it can be overpowering, so just use a drop.

> *Fill my want,*
> *Know what I need*
> *Inspired by fire*
> *From shyness freed.*
>
> *Let touch take us*
> *To a newfound place*
> *On a sphere that blazes*
> *Its way through space.*

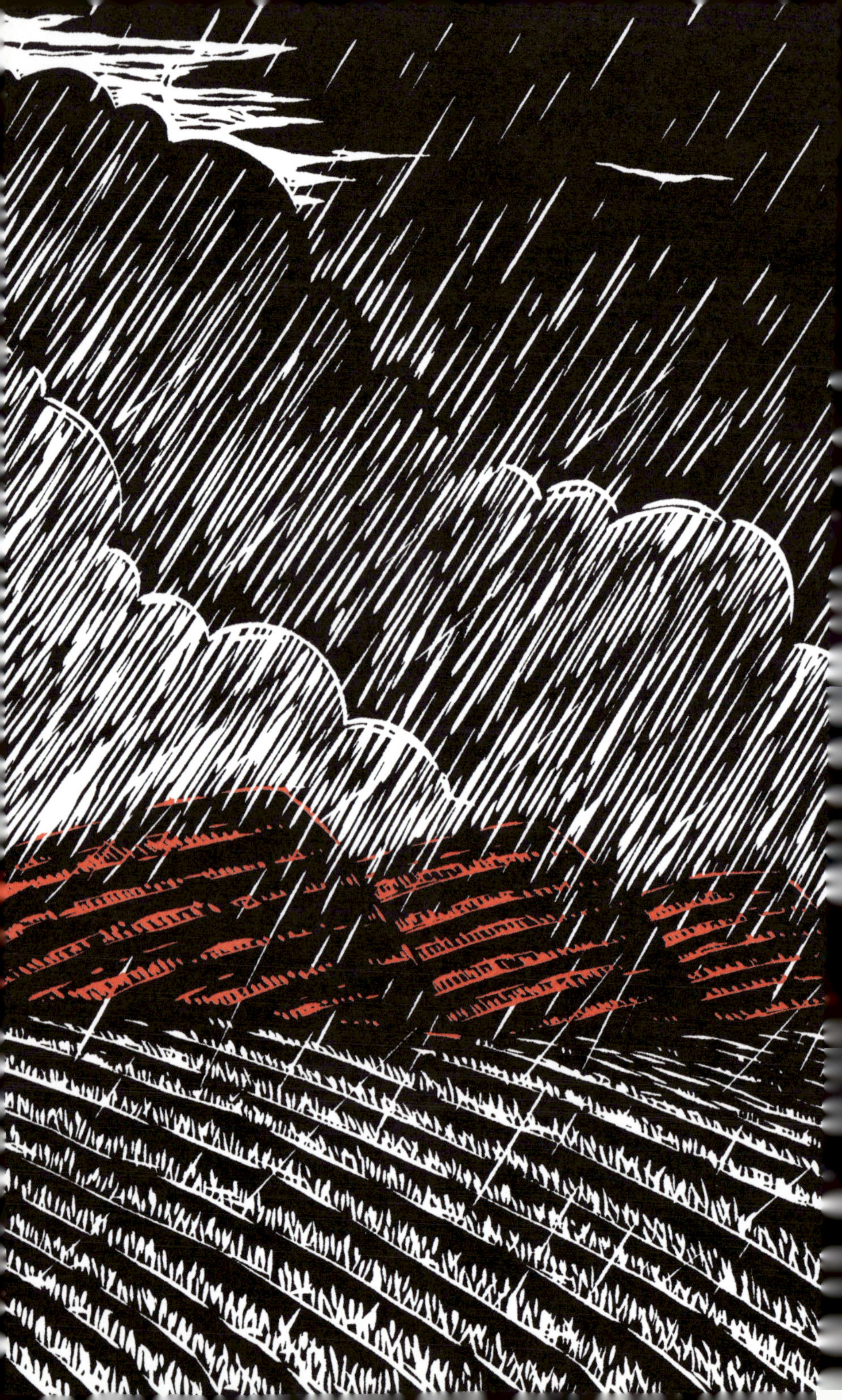

SPELLS TO DISPEL TROUBLE AND MAKE LOVE LAST

TO HELP BOND YOU WITH SOMEONE
TRADITIONAL

To make a romantic partner feel bonded to you, use this Gaelic charm. Keep a sprig of mint in your hand till the herb grows moist and warm, then take hold of the hand of the woman you love, and she will follow you as long as the two hands close over the herb. No invocation is necessary, but silence must be kept between the two parties for ten minutes, to give the charm time to work with due efficacy.

TO MAKE LOVE LAST
TRADITIONAL

Love will last forever with this charm. Take a bay leaf and split it in half. Kneel with your beloved in front of a red candle. Kiss one half of the bay leaf, then press the other side to their mouth to kiss. They should repeat the same process with the other bay leaf half. Tie the two halves together with one strand of hair from each of your heads. Place it in a green sachet and bury in your yard or another place that has meaning for you.

FOR STRONG LONG-DISTANCE RELATIONSHIPS
JAMES BENJAMIN KENYON

Go to a body of water and find a smooth rock or shell. Write your name on one side, and your beloved's name on the other. Throw the rock or shell into the water and recite:

> *My love is like the vastness of the sea,*
> *As deep as life, as high as heaven is high,*
> *And pure as an unclouded summer sky.*

LONG-LASTING LOVE POTION
GABRIEL GREY

To make love last, place a diamond and a pearl in spring water for seven hours. Remove them, and then drink the water with your love. Tell each other why you love each other. You should perform this spell after a fight or during a new moon.

TO MAKE SURE SOMEONE STAYS FAITHFUL
TRADITIONAL

In order to make sure your partner stays faithful to you, sew the feather of a swan into the seam of his pillow and he will never stray.

FOR NEW LONG-LASTING LOVE
ELISA SHOENBERGER

This spell is to bring someone new into your life whom you'll have a long-lasting love with. You will need:

Ink

Quill

2 long ribbons

1 key (not to a current lock).

Perform this spell at midnight when the moon is waxing. Take the ink and quill and begin writing your name on one of the ribbons. You only need to write your name on one side. On the other ribbon write, "My love."

Once the ink has dried on both ribbons, begin braiding them together to make a single ribbon. While braiding, chant:

> *May this ribbon signed*
> *Be ever intertwined*
> *With the cord and line*
> *Of my love now to find.*

Next, thread the braided ribbon through the key. Tie the ribbon and key into a circle and chant:

> *I ask that this braided key*
> *Reveal my new love to me.*

Place the ribbon into a purse or backpack that you carry with you.

LOVING HOME RITUAL
JILL ROBI

First cleanse the home by smudging sage in all rooms and corridors. Then chant, *This house will be full of love*, as you anoint each door and entryway with a natural-hair paintbrush. To make this blessed oil mixture, use cinnamon, clover, dragon's blood, and frankincense.

NEW HOME BLESSING
DY EDWARDS

Before you go inside,
And scatter your furniture, nesting like you belong here,
Decide which of your demons to leave behind,
Remember that all homes have a heart,
And you may need some time to find this one.

If the house is old, it has maybe seen too much,
But it knows how humans work,
Talk respectfully to it, introduce yourself,
As with any meeting, this is best done over tea,
It will come to understand if you let it.

If your house is new, speak softly,
It may need coaxing to come out at all,
It may be quiet, skittish, and small,
Uncertain of everything and afraid of your darkness,
It won't know what it's expected to do yet,
It's okay for you to explain.

First for a blessing,
Spray the walls with rosewater,
(Lavender, violet, sandalwood, or Florida water
    also suffice).
Dilute with plain water and a touch of white vinegar,
(It will work if it feels like home to you).
Wipe away the drips and any debris they dredge up,
Scatter salt over the floors.
Tell it to clear away any hidden grime or old grudges,

SPELLS TO DISPEL TROUBLE AND MAKE LOVE LAST

Vacuum it up again.
Witches are feared and powerful,
    and the worst are the best,
So remember: the worst witches are the kind who clean.

Second, you will need something that smokes.
If you know a cedar tree, ask it nicely if you
    can take an old dry branch
(offer it water to sweeten the deal).
If you don't, take Palo Santo, or incense
(Sage works if you can find it,
But mind where it was harvested).

Enter your home again and leave the front door ajar
    behind you.
Walk until you find the farthest, darkest corner
(it's usually upstairs).
Speak to any spirits you find.
Let them know who you are,
And let them decide if they want to stay.
If they do, this is a good time to set house rules—
Help protect what I have, what I'll make.
Help yourself to the last glass of wine
Or any unattended cookies.
Please don't tease the cat too much, she's getting old—
If they need help to leave instead, listen to what they
    need and do your best for them.
If they won't leave and move to strike you or yours,
Remember *worst is best*
The worst witches are the kind who clean.

LOVE MAGIC

When the right deals are made,
And the house is on your side,
Light your smoke.
Let it drift through the house and
    wave it out the windows.
Let it enter your lungs and be expelled with your
    worries.
Send it and them out the front door.
The ashes of your enemies should be swept up
    as you go.
If they left any marks,
You may need more salt,
Or a touch of peroxide.
When all this is done, wash the smog off the windows.

Gather your spirits again,
And any you befriended.
Sit at the hearth with a candle and a pot of tea
(some spirits will want coffee instead—
the best hosts are flexible).
Ask for their stories;
Laugh at their jokes;
Tell your own.
Bless the home and its guests with laughter,
With joy,
With warmth.
Let the spirits crowd around you,
Then let them disperse.

Look around your quiet, empty house.
Remember whatever you left behind.
Let yourself grieve if you must,
But do not linger.
Move along. Move along.
Move along.

As you move in,
Find homes for your furniture.
Your pictures, your altar.
Listen to the house if it gives suggestions.
It knows itself better than you,
But leave space for yourself.

One day the spirits will come round again;
They'll remember your gifts and your joy;
They'll return whatever you gave,
And without quite realizing how
You'll find yourself home again.

WATER SPELL
DES D. WILSON

For this protection spell, gather:
- 1 bowl
- Clean and drinkable water
- Bay leaves
- Large, green palm leaf
- Blue or white candle

Water is life. We take it for granted in the Western world that there will always be plentiful, safe water to drink. But this need not be the case at all, as many people around the world unfortunately know all too well. This spell harnesses the power of this precious liquid to protect your beloved from want. Use it especially whenever they are in need, like when money is tight or a job is lost. First, collect some water yourself; pour some in a small bowl, and make sure you can see the water when casting the spell. All around the bowl, place a good number of bay leaves—they must completely surround the bowl. Place the palm leaf in front of the bowl and bay leaves. The palm leaf will transform into a shield protecting your beloved from harm. Finally, light the candle while uttering the following words:

> *Precious and pure, to drink and to sate,*
> *water will [your beloved's name] never forsake.*
> *Protect [him/her] from need, from want, and from grief,*
> *May the fullest of cups provide best relief.*

PEACEFUL HOME CHARM
TRADITIONAL

Burn lavender or lavender-scented incense around your home, especially in doorways and windows. This will ensure that only good spirits visit your home and that those who dwell there and visit don't leave too much negative energy.

GERANIUM CHARM
ANASTASIA GREYWOLF

Write your name and your lover's on a piece of paper and bury it in a pot of soil. Plant geranium seeds on top of it. When you plant the seeds and every time you water them, think loving thoughts about your significant other and yourself. While you water, take turns reading a book aloud to each other. When the plant blooms, pick its first bloom and press it in the book. Keep the dried, pressed flower for good luck in your relationship.

TO GET ALONG WITH YOUR IN-LAWS
GEMMA ARONSON

Are your in-laws annoying? Do you want them to like you more? Do you need more harmony in your relationship? This ancient spell will charm them in whatever way you wish.

You will need:

1 small glass jar with a metal lid

Honey

Brown paper

1 pencil

Heather or lavender flowers or oil

1 purple candle.

Fill your small glass jar to the top with honey. Tear your brown paper into a square and write your in-laws' first and last names on it. Rotate the paper one turn clockwise and write your first and last name across their names twice, so your name crisscrosses theirs. If there is only one in-law, write your and their name just once.

Write your request or wish in a circle around all the names; the pencil must not leave the paper so that the request is one continuous loop. Practice this a few times. If you make a mistake on your paper, start again.

Fold the paper in half three times, and say your request aloud during each fold. Each fold must be done toward you.

Rub your flowers or oil lightly along your candle and light it.

Now take a spoonful of honey from the jar and eat it. Chant the following three times if you want them to like you more:

> *As this honey sweetens me*
> *So will [insert in-laws' names]*
>   *be as sweet to me*

If you want them to appear less annoying, chant the following three times:

> *As this honey sweetens me*
> *So will [insert in-laws' names] seem to me*

Now place the folded paper into your jar. Push it all the way in so that it's covered in honey and tighten the metal lid.

Seal the lid all the way around with melted wax from your candle. Now place the candle securely on top of your jar and let the candle burn out to the end.

TO PREVENT SOMEONE FROM LEAVING
TRADITIONAL

You can't (or shouldn't) *really* prevent someone from leaving, but this charm will give them second thoughts right as they're about to leave. Use that opportunity well.

You will need pieces of cloth torn from clothes the person has worn. In a bucket of spring water, add several drops of clove, sage, and jasmine oil. Add the cloth and let it sit for seven hours. Use the cloth to rub the water all over doorways and doors (even car doors).

TO FIX LOVE GONE WRONG
ANASTASIA GREYWOLF

On a white piece of paper with blue ink, write down what you feel has gone wrong in your relationship. Find a seashell and place it inside; leave the seashell where you found it. If your relationship has multiple problems, use multiple pieces of paper and multiple seashells. Obtain a white rose, and take a petal off the rose each day while accessing your hopes for a peaceful resolution. When you run out of petals, return to the seashells. If the notes or shells are gone, the situation with your lover will improve. If not, you will have to accept the problems or move on.

TO SEPARATE TWO LOVERS
TRADITIONAL

If the one you love is with another, you can speak aloud this old Cherokee shaman spell.

> *Yû! On high you repose, O Blue Hawk, there at the far distant lake. The blue tobacco has come to be your recompense. Now you have arisen at once and come down. You have alighted midway between them where they two are standing. You have spoiled their souls immediately. They have at once become separated.*

TO MAKE SOMEONE TELL THE TRUTH
KATRIEL WINTERS

Light a brown, red, or yellow candle. White will also work if you cannot find the other colors. If you have a larger candle, this spell can be repeated over several days if desired, lighting and relighting as needed. Take whole cloves or peppercorns, spread them along with kosher salt on a small saucer or tin, and say: *The Truth will out, or may the teller stumble.*

TRUTH SERUM
TRADITIONAL

In order to induce a person to tell the truth in any manner, take the dirt from inside of their shoes and grind it with passion flower. Place it in a bottle of whiskey, adding more dirt and passion flower every three days for twenty-one days. One drop on the tongue will cause the person to be unable to tell a lie for several minutes. Let the whiskey serum continue to age to prolong the effects.

RELATIONSHIP RESCUE PIE
JILL ROBI

When things are going sour in your relationship, sweeten things up with Relationship Rescue Pie. You will need:

- 2 prepared piecrusts
- 4 Granny Smith apples, peeled and quartered
- ⅔ cup packed dark brown sugar
- ½ teaspoon ground cinnamon
- ½ teaspon ground nutmeg
- ¼ teaspoon ground cloves
- ¼ teaspoon salt
- 1 tablespoon all-purpose flour
- 2 tablespoons unsalted butter, at room temperature, cut into ½-inch pieces

1 egg white, beaten until frothy

2 tablespoons chopped pecans

1 can cherry pie filling

Preheat the oven to 400°F. Cut the apple quarters into wedges of three, and mix in a medium bowl with the sugar, cinnamon, nutmeg, salt, flour, and butter.

Place one piecrust in a pie pan and brush the inside of the crust with the beaten egg whites. Trim the excess crust. Pour the apple filling into the crust.

Cut the center out of the remaining piecrust, and place it on top, folding the edges. Brush with the remaining egg-white mixture. Add three dollops of the cherry pie filling into the center, and sprinkle the chopped pecans on top. (Note: If allergic to nuts, use a rolled oats mixture to add texture for the topping.)

Bake for about one hour until the crust is a deep, golden brown. Let cool for 30 minutes, then slice and serve!

FOR A PEACEFUL RELATIONSHIP
SAVANA LEE

Imbue your relationship with energies of peaceful harmony and light. Here is a spell to banish discord and feel love renewed within your home.

LOVE MAGIC

You will need:

- 1 sage stick or Palo Santo
- 1 white or pink candle
- 2 small pieces of white paper (write your name on one and the name of your beloved on the other)
- 1 small white ribbon
- A wooden tray or altar

Perform this spell when the moon is waxing, preferably the last three nights up to or including the full moon. The moon in the sign of Taurus will add extra strength and vibrancy to your long-term relationship energies. You may perform the spell during any moon sign other than Taurus; just be aware it may require more focus and concentration.

As you set your ingredients on your tray or altar, envision in your mind what harmony and peace mean to you. This may look like a cease in anger, projection, or conflict. It may look like tranquility or connection between you and your partner. Sometimes even a beautiful landscape will appear to symbolize the deepening of intimacy and peace. Hold whatever arises for you in your mind and heart. Light your candle and then your sage stick from your candle. Smudge your body, your ingredients, and altar from left to right. Turn your altar so that it faces east.

SPELLS TO DISPEL TROUBLE AND MAKE LOVE LAST

Call in the Quarters, starting with the East, to build your sacred ritual circle. Recite the following words: *I call in Energy of the East and guidance of the Air Element for protection and strength.*

Turn clockwise as you call the energies of Love and Peace toward you and recite again: *I call in the Energy of the South and Fire Element for protection and strength.*

Repeat again clockwise for the Energy of the West and Water and finally for the North and Earth. Turn clockwise one last time and face your altar.

Take the papers with both names and turn them so the names face each other. Fold them together three times. Recite these words aloud:

> *My will is that my partner and I thrive in an environment of peace and unity. May our connection and intimacy grow as strong as vines from the deep Earth, wholly intertwined, while old grudges and arguments fall away with the wind. I reawaken the fire of love running solidly beneath us and reaffirm our commitment. I call in harmony with my beloved and bring our bond into the light. So mote it be.*

Wrap your papers with the white ribbon and tie if possible. Thank the elements for their guidance and protection and declare your sacred circle closed. Place your ribbon-wrapped names beneath the bed you and your partner share on a night you will both be sleeping there. You may find you dream of love, tranquil landscapes, and/or the face of your beloved. Repeat as needed to strengthen your relationship and bring harmony into your home.

FOR HARMONY IN A HOUSEHOLD
M. D. MCDUFF

Use this spell to imbibe small tokens with peace to maintain harmony in your home.

First, gather objects representing each family member. Some suggestions are stones or pebbles, seashells, or other small, unassuming objects. When selecting these objects, focus on each item individually and visualize the family member the item represents. Choose an object for yourself as well.

Pour clean, cold water into a bowl, and take it to the eastern corner of your home. Add violets for luck and protection. Add lavender for peace. Then add dill to provide power against evil forces. (You can use essential oil instead if available.) Wash each object that you have selected to represent your family members in the water and then arrange these items around the bowl. Continue moving them until you feel like they are placed correctly. Focus on each object, first individually, and then focus on the picture in front of you as a whole. Envision your family and speak these words:

Harmony, I invite you into my home.
Peace, please come to stay.
Protect us. Keep us calm.
Infuse these items on this day.

Take the items and put them somewhere inside your home, either all together or in separate places, wherever they make the most sense to you. Periodically touch the items, thinking of your family and remembering the spell.

The spell may wear off over time. Feel free to repeat it with the same items representing your family.

TO RELEASE NEGATIVE ENERGY
ANASTASIA GREYWOLF

Write with blue ink on a white piece of paper:

I release [name of person]
From my negative energy
And will harness only the positive energy around us.

Fold the piece of paper one time, and place it under a vase of white flowers. When the flowers wilt, burn the note and burn the ashes with the dead flowers and a clove of garlic far away from your home.

AFTER-FIGHT CLEANSING CHARM
TRADITIONAL

Open all the windows and doors. Sprinkle saltwater in the corners of each room and in any areas where fighting occurred. Take a piece of white cloth, and holding two corners, sweep it through the air, moving the air and energy toward the open windows and doors. Then light sage leaves or sage incense, and repeat the same process, focusing again on the areas where arguing occurred.

SPELLS TO DISPEL TROUBLE AND MAKE LOVE LAST

◆ TO MAKE A LOVER COME BACK
TRADITIONAL

If a maid wishes to see her lover, let her use the following method: Prick the third or wedding finger of your left hand with a sharp needle (beware a pin), and with the blood, write your own and your lover's name on a piece of clean writing paper, in as small a compass as you can, and encircle it with three round rings of the same crimson stream. Fold it up, and exactly at the ninth hour of the evening, bury it with your own hand in the earth, and tell no one. Your lover will hasten to you as soon as possible, and (if you have quarreled) makes up. A young man may also try this charm, only instead of the wedding finger, let him pierce the left thumb.

SECOND-CHANCE LOVE SPELL
ELISIA G

Ahh, regret. What do you do when a good person has exited your life and you realize afterwards how much that relationship actually meant to you? This spell is to be executed only after the dust has cleared from any fights or fallouts. It must be entered with a clear head and firm grip on reality: you should only do it if you're certain that you've evolved beyond whatever mistake or mindset you had when this person left. After all, if it works, they will be around for good!

That being said, the first part of this spell is to make your stance crystal clear in your own mind. Take a quartz crystal and set it on a blank piece of paper with a pen or pencil nearby. Let the crystal charge the writing space for at least twenty-four hours. When you're ready, sit down and begin. Tarot cards are listed for your reference.

Establish a clear mind: How have you evolved since you were last with this person? What clarity and perspec-

SPELLS TO DISPEL TROUBLE AND MAKE LOVE LAST

tive are you bringing to this new stage of the relationship? Make a list of all the traits you've acquired or faced head-on within yourself—in short, your own evolution and enlightenment—in order to enter stage two with a clean slate. Tarot card: Judgment.

Express your clear heart: What do you love about this person? What do you love about yourself with this person? Write it out. This is also the time to get out any lingering resentment or anger you have toward this person. Tarot card: Six of Hearts.

Ask the universe for help: Acknowledge that this second chance isn't wholly within your control; you're going to need some help from the powers that be. Ask the universe clearly for an opportunity that will allow you to rekindle your old flame. Timing is everything, and in order for this to work you will need some inspired intervention. It also prevents you from desperately chasing after your lost love. Tarot card: Ace of Wands.

Once you've written out your intentions, fold the paper up and place it in a safe space. To anchor your intention, replace the crystal with a rock you like. Choose something that represents that lucky opportunity—a stopwatch, a match, a clover—and place it with your letter as well. Then walk away, clearing that person from your mind as much as possible. Go about your days with a clear head and heart—do *not* chase that person—so that they will instead come to you when the time is right.

TO MAKE SOMEONE FALL IN LOVE WITH YOU AGAIN
GRETA GOLDBART

Take a piece of paper with the handwriting of the one lost. Sleep with it under your pillow for three nights. On the fourth night, light a red candle, and in front of it, speak these words:

And so what was lost shall return. Repeat this phrase thrice. Then, fold the piece of paper so that you can drip the wax of the candle onto it, creating a seal, as if the paper was an envelope.

Once the wax has hardened, replace it under your pillow, and sleep with it there for three more nights. The morning after the third night, remove the paper, and open the seal. Carry the paper around in a pocket, purse, or wallet, and the lost love will return.

TO KEEP YOUR LOVER SAFE
MARGUERITE WILKINSON

To keep your love safe, find a quiet place where you can focus your energy on them, and recite the following (replacing "her" for "him" if desired).

O great sun of heaven, harm not my love;
Sear him not with your flame,
  blind him not with your beauty,
Shine for his pleasure!

O gray rains of heaven, harm not my love;
Drown not in your torrent the song of his heart,
Lave and caress him.

O swift winds of heaven, harm not my love;
Bruise not nor buffet him with your rough humor,
Sing you his prowess!

O mighty triad, strong ones of heaven,
Sun, rain, and wind, be gentle, I charge you—
For your mad mood of wrath have me—I am ready—
But spare him, my lover, most proud and most dear,
O sun, rain and wind, strong ones of heaven!

TO PROTECT YOUR LOVE FROM PHYSICAL HARM
DES D. WILSON

If you are concerned that your lover could be harmed physically, whether by accident or intentional violence, you can protect them using this powerful spell. First, calm your mind by sitting quietly in a secluded spot; simply focus on your breath for about five minutes. Picture your beloved in your mind. Then, when you are feeling quite settled, light three green candles—the green color represents the boundlessness of the earth that contains every living thing, including your lover—on an elevated surface such as a small table or stool. In front or beneath the lit candles, place a bowl of clean water and two large green palm leaves. The palm leaves will become shields conferring invulnerability to your beloved, and the water serves as a channel to communicate and amplify your spell throughout the universe. Repeat the following mantra for five minutes without pause: *Protect [your beloved's name] from all harm, whether human or natural. Let no harm come to [him/her]. This shield will not break. Within it [he/she] is safe.* If, for whatever reason, you find yourself continually worrying about the physical safety of your partner, then it's also a good idea to gift them an emerald or black onyx, which are very effective protective stones.

OLD-WORLD FERTILITY CHARM
TRADITIONAL

To conceive a child, try this old European remedy. Have a fertile woman drink the water in which the husband has spit, while reciting: *Where I am flame, be thou the coals. Where I am rain, be thou the water!*

FERTILITY SPELL
M. D. MCDUFF

This is a spell to increase your fertility and prepare you to carry a child. You will need:

   1 white candle

   1 bowl

   A knife

   Ground cinnamon

   Ylang-ylang, orange, or sandalwood essential oil

   At least two of the following offerings: grapes, carrot, pumpkin, wheat, apple, banana, avocado, and cucumber

Before you say the fertility spell, you must first cleanse your mind and your body. Prepare a bath. The temperature is unimportant, but be sure it is a temperature that makes you feel comfortable. Next to your bath, light one white candle.

The sacral chakra is the one connected to your reproductive organs. To help cleanse this chakra, add ylang-ylang, orange, or sandalwood essential oil to your bath water. If more than one of these oils is available to you, inhale them each, one at a time, and decide if you want to use just one or a combination. For best results, make this decision immediately before your bath, not in advance. You may also diffuse any of these oils in the room while you bathe.

LOVE MAGIC

While bathing, clear your mind. Take deep, calming breaths. Relax. Focus on your intention. When you are ready, drain your bath water. Blow out your candle.

Prepare your offering, which may contain grapes, carrots, pumpkin, wheat, an apple, a banana, an avocado, and/or a cucumber. Again, choose whichever ones you are drawn to, but be sure to include at least two. All of these items represent the fruits of the earth and symbolize fertility.

Wash your selections carefully, and cut them into pieces as if you were going to eat them. Mix the pieces together in a bowl.

Go outside and select a tree. Birch, hawthorn, oak, pine, or any nut-bearing tree works best. If trees are not available, try to find daffodils, geraniums, or sunflowers.

Cast your protection circle: sprinkle ground cinnamon in a circle encompassing you and the tree. Be sure to leave enough room for you to sit.

Sit down with your bowl. Close your eyes. Keep at least one hand on the bowl. The other hand can touch the bowl, the tree or flower, or the ground. Focus again on your intention. Think about the love and protection you will have for your future child. Think about the home you will create for your child. Feel love and peace.

When you are ready, take a deep breath and repeat these words three times:

> *Oh, holy mother, your spirit wild*
> *I am ready to bear a precious child.*
> *My deepest desire, I sit here professing*
> *With this offering, bestow your blessing*

As you complete the spell the third time, pour your offering onto the roots of the tree.

TO PROTECT A BABY YET TO BE BORN
TRADITIONAL

To protect an unborn child, encase a branch of myrtle in a soft cloth. Place candles in a pentagram shape around the cloth. Recite five times:

> *By Eileithyia, by Hera, learn your mother's words from her own mouth, baby, come forth so that we may hear thy cry.*

BLESSING FOR A NEW BABY
DY EDWARDS

As a blessing for a new baby, recite the following:

Strawberry, fennel, and fern,
Give me the strength to carry on
Ease our burdens as you may
Let me heal so they can grow.
Child, may I have the strength to carry you
May you arrive safe, on time, and hale
May I not forget to care for myself—
I need all my strength for you

Peppermint, cabbage, and rose,
Give me the calm and wisdom all parents find
Let our pains be few and passing
Help me let go so they can grow.
Child, may you grow quickly and safely
May the world rise up at your feet
May you always know what is rightness
May you never falter on your path

Hazel, wolf's milk, and thyme,
Protect our spirits and our home
As I teach my child the world I know
May they in turn show me the world as they grow.
Child, may you find wonder and joy
May you know more love than pain
May you have the strength to fight—
And the compassion to know when

Later we'll call rosemary, cypress, and sage
For all parents must part from their children
Leaving memory, loving, and tears
But as the world turns, we both will remember
The strawberry, fennel, and fern.

TO PROTECT YOUR FAMILY
ELISA SHOENBERGER

This spell is intended to protect your family, including your children. You will need:

Sprigs of lavender

Basil leaves

A family photo

Perform the spell in the morning as the sun is rising. Gather sprigs of the lavender and basil with the photo. Chant four times, once in each cardinal direction:

Come sun up, come sun down
East, West, North, South, all around
May upon my beloved family ward
Bring us health, happiness, and accord

Perform the spell again in the afternoon. Perform the spell for a final time at night when the moon is out.

Put the photo into a frame. Dry the lavender. Once dried, place the flowers with the photo.

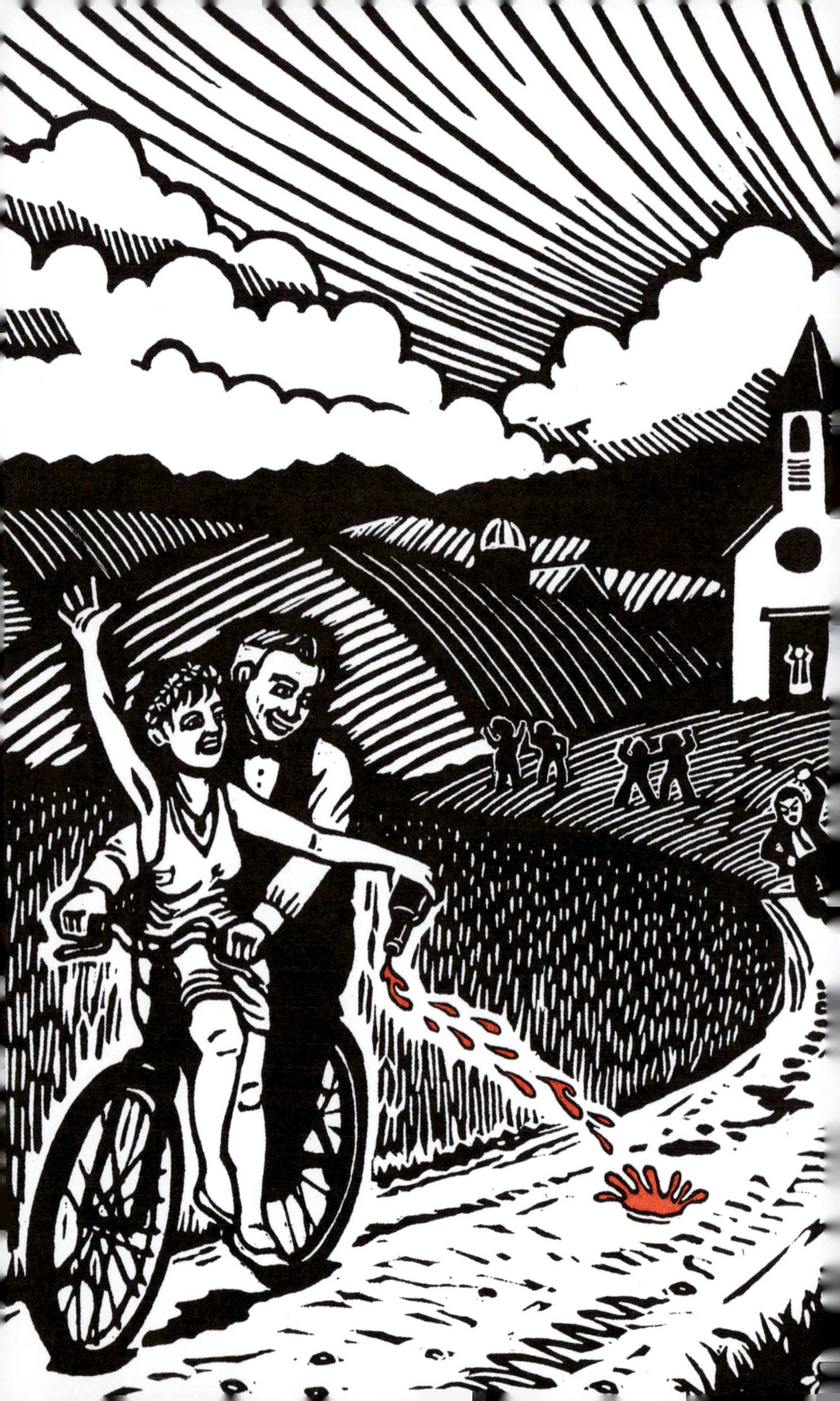

SPELLS AND BLESSINGS FOR MARRIAGE AND ENGAGEMENTS

NINETY-NINE HORSES (AND A MULE) CHARM
TRADITIONAL

One way to ensure a particular person will become your spouse is to look upon ninety-nine different horses, and then one white mule. Immediately after seeing the mule, shake your intended's hand, and you will one day be married.

TO MARRY WHOMEVER YOU CHOOSE
TRADITIONAL

To make the person you love want to marry you and ensure a union, the solution is simple. Obtain the heart of a chicken and swallow it whole.

TO KNOW IF YOU SHOULD GET MARRIED
TRADITIONAL

If you receive a proposal but aren't sure if you should accept it, take several hairs from your head and place them on a piece of paper with several hairs from a cat. Fold the paper in half and place it under your doormat overnight. In the morning, if they are in a straight line, the answer is no. If they are form a pattern on the paper, the answer is yes.

TO GET A MARRIAGE PROPOSAL
LUNA ETERNAL

You will need:

> Something personal belonging to your love (hair works best)
>
> A white cloth
>
> Rose oil
>
> A simple band (can be a ring or something as simple as a piece of string tied to fit your finger)
>
> 1 red candle
>
> A red ribbon.

Place your love's hair or personal item onto the center of the cloth. Pour the rose oil onto the item. Place the band on top and repeat this incantation three times:

> *With the love that is ours*
> *I call upon this ancient power*
> *Engagement is what I seek*
> *Proposal is what you offer to me*
> *By the power of three times three*
> *As I will it, so mote it be!*

After it has been said, seal the items together using the red candle wax. Once completely covered, gather the ends of the cloth together and using the ribbon tie the ends, creating a small "sack."

The next time you are in your love's house, place the small bundle under the bed. You should have a proposal within the month!

TO GET SOMEONE TO ACCEPT A MARRIAGE PROPOSAL
TRADITIONAL

To get someone to accept your marriage proposal, take an unworn gold ring studded with a small diamond. Wrap it in a piece of green fabric, and for nine days and nine nights wear it against your heart. On the ninth day, before the sun rises, have the word "Scheva" engraved inside the ring by someone who is a new engraver. Obtain three hairs from the person you want to love you, and tie them together with three of your own around the ring while saying:

> *Body, that you could love me, that your desires could be as passionate as mine, by Scheva's most potent virtue.*

Then wrap the ring in a piece of silk, and wear it against your heart for another six days. On the seventh day, unwrap the ring and give it to the person you desire.

If your ring is accepted, then you can be certain to be loved by that person. If the ring is refused, rest assured that the heart of that person belongs to another and in that case, you should seek love elsewhere.

A CHARM FOR WRITING YOUR VOWS
SAVANA LEE

This charm will bring forth your truest vows and shower blessings upon all your wedding activities. Create your charm during the waxing moon, up to and including the full moon, to bring energies of nurturing and abundance to your spell.

Gather pictures of both you and your betrothed and a small charm to carry (any kind of copper, silver, or gold, if you prefer), shaped in an image that calls to your soul. Some have chosen a heart, flower, cross, or sentimental jewel. A word of caution: if you choose a family heirloom, do not use another's wedding ring for this charm. Ideally, the heirloom or jewel will be cleansed beforehand in a mixture of baking soda, hot water, and dish soap, as well as smudged by the light of a new moon to clear away any old energies.

Light a white or rose candle and then a Palo Santo or your smudge stick from the candle. Smudge your body and items, especially your charm, from left to right.

Close your eyes and pass the charm over both the pictures of you and your betrothed. Pause for a moment over each and imagine your long and beautiful adventure in life together. Recite the following aloud:

> *May this charm bring forth the eloquence and truest words to express my love. I know I will be guided to*

write vows that honor the love I am committed to giving and receiving in this life. May my guardians and the Elements bless this charm and my marriage with the highest light and good for myself and [the name of your betrothed]. May this charm be infused with all the energies of balance, true love, honesty, and fidelity.* May it guide me through the following days and through the bliss of my wedding day as I step onto my path as a life partner. Thank you for the blessings and guidance I receive this day and every day.

Carry your charm with you as you sit down to write your vows, through all your pre-wedding activities, and even through the ceremony if you wish. May your journey of love and commitment be a blessed and beautiful one.

* You may add to or change this list as necessary. Some suggestions are fertility, fortune, abundance, security, health, or any other defining feature you believe will enhance the journey of your marriage.

PRE-WEDDING BATH
JILL ROBI

Light pillar candles for each corner of your bathtub. As the water runs, anoint it with a few drops of jasmine and myrtle oil. Add drops of ylang-ylang and orange blossom oils. Once it's full, scatter red and pink rose petals on top. While taking this special wedding bath, meditate, thinking of the best version of your special day, pulling positive energy into yourself, and projecting that into the universe.

TO CURE PRE-WEDDING JITTERS
ANASTASIA GREYWOLF

If you find yourself suffering from pre-wedding jitters, it is best to be in the company of another witch. If there isn't another witch nearby, a good friend will do. Light a candle (any color but black) and hold both hands with person and be silent. Breathe in through your nose and out through your mouth slowly 5 times. On the first time, think about your legs. On the second time, think about your torso. On the third, your chest and heart, on the forth, your head. On the fifth, open your eyes. You will know in your heart if you want to continue on with your wedding day. If you do, play your favorite song and dance around the candle with your companion, thinking of nothing but your happy life with your future spouse. If you don't, blow out the candle. Then (as long as it is cool enough), pour the melted wax from the candle onto your skin, which will give you the strength to call off the wedding.

GOOD LUCK WEDDING CHARM
ANASTASIA GREYWOLF

Make a circle with alternating blue and white candles. Place a photo of you and your spouse-to-be in the center. You, your partner, and even other loved ones should stand in front of the circle and project good intentions and love. Each person should say something positive about the couple that will make them strong and lasting partners. Then everyone should blow out the candles at the same time.

A TALISMAN FOR A HEARTFELT WEDDING
JEANNE DE LA WARE

This two-step ritual is for those who worry that stage fright, the logistics of hosting wedding guests, or other distractions will intrude into their thoughts during the marriage ceremony, taking focus away from the meaning of the moment. It involves creating a talisman for clear-seeing and depth of experience, which you will carry during the ceremony in a pocket or attached to a bouquet.

You will need a paper copy of a photograph or drawing of you and your intended in a joyful or tender moment, rose essential oil (associated with gratitude, love, and passion), and a short length of brown ribbon (associated with new beginnings, grounding, and security).

Step one: On the back of the photo, write two or more hopes for your marriage and intentions toward your beloved.

Step two: Recite the following, while anointing each corner of the paper with the rose oil:

LOVE MAGIC

> *Diamonds and garnets,*
> *calendula, birch;*
> *In nature, home, town hall,*
> *in temple or church,*
>
> *wherever we gather,*
> *and our two selves present*
> *to be joined together*
> *so we cannot be rent:*

Now, roll up the paper while reciting:

> *Lavender, rosemary,*
> *copper, and pearl,*
> *quiet the noise*
> *of the rest of the world.*
>
> *Let us marvel, be awed*
> *at the change that is nigh.*
> *Let us see our beloveds*
> *with a clear, tender eye.*

Now recite, while tying the ribbon around the paper

> *Cyclamen, lapis,*
> *moonstone, and phlox,*
> *take all distractions*
> *away from our thoughts.*
>
> *Narrow our vision,*
> *so we only perceive*
> *the shower of blessings*
> *we are about to receive.*

FOR A WEDDING DAY THAT IS FREE OF CONFLICT
SUSAN ADCOX

Wedding spells are traditionally used any time after lovers are pledged to one another. There is no need to wait until the actual wedding day. This type of wedding spell, which is directed toward a smooth and strife-free joining, can be cast at any time during the planning process. Make the most of this ritual by creating a ritual space and doing it nightly. Since the purpose is to maintain the sweetness of the occasion, you can place a jar of honey, a sweet-smelling flower such as jasmine or honeysuckle, or an aromatic herb such as lavender in your space. If you use this spell at bedtime, your sleep will also be sweetened as you will be relieved of worries about your wedding day. Recite:

> *If tempers are short, please soothe them.*
> *If nerves are frayed, please smooth them.*
> *If a heart holds envy, replace it.*
> *If a soul shelters anger, erase it.*
> *If a tongue tries to wag, please bind it.*
> *If our hearts need peace, let us find it.*
> *Let all good portents wing their way*
> *To bless us on our coupling day.*

FOR GOOD WEATHER ON YOUR WEDDING DAY
JILL ROBI

Eight days before your wedding day, take a light green candle and drop three drops of almond oil on the top to charge it. Thinking of the kind of weather that you want, light the candle. Close your eyes and meditate, focusing on that specific type of weather. After seven minutes, blow the candle out and say, *So mote it be*. Do this for the next seven days.

WEDDING WALNUT CHARM
TRADITIONAL

At nighttime during the full moon before your wedding, you and your spouse-to-be should take two shelled walnuts and use them to write each other's initials in the ground under the oldest tree you can find. Then bury the walnuts together under the tree.

WEDDING LOVE SPELL
ELISA SHOENBERGER

This spell aims to maintain (or increase) the love you feel on your wedding day so that it continues unbroken after your marriage.

SPELLS AND BLESSINGS FOR MARRIAGE AND ENGAGEMENTS

You will need several sprigs of an evergreen tree, a small glass of honey, and your wedding (or engagement) rings. Perform the spell a few nights before the wedding, preferably when the moon is waxing.

Take several sprigs of evergreen and arrange them in a circle. Place the small glass with honey in the middle. Hold the rings above the evergreen and honey and chant:

> *With these rings exchanged between*
> *Our love shall grow evergreen*
> *From lip to lip, may each kiss*
> *Taste of aged honey of shared bliss*

Kiss the rings and place them into the evergreen ring. Take the evergreen sprigs and spread them throughout your wedding flowers, like table arrangements and other decorations, to extend the goodwill.

TO PREVENT FAMILY MEMBERS FROM RUINING A WEDDING
M. D. MCDUFF

For this spell you will need:

> Agrimony: to avoid bad energy or hexes
>
> Bergamot: for instinctual luck
>
> Basil: to chase away melancholy, remove obstacles, and encourage harmony
>
> Bay leaves: to banish ill will
>
> Blueberry: to prevent treachery from loved ones
>
> Geranium: for banishing negativity; for protection, love, and healing
>
> Lavender: for peace, to shield from negativity
>
> Peppermint: to create change and get things moving
>
> Vetiver: for protection, cleansing, and refocusing; greatest for unhexing

The ingredients work best when fresh, but can be used dried when needed. A single drop of an essential oil can be used in place of the ingredient if fresh or dried cannot be found. Each herb should be torn into small pieces or ground up by either the bride or the groom. Either the bride or the groom, or both together, should handle the ingredients and mix the potion.

Boil water in a small pot. Once boiling, lower the heat. Do not allow the water to be hotter than a simmer.

SPELLS AND BLESSINGS FOR MARRIAGE AND ENGAGEMENTS

First, add the agrimony. Let sit for five minutes before adding any other ingredients. Then, add the basil. Again, let sit for five minutes before adding any other ingredients. Stir periodically with a cinnamon stick.

Increase the heat. Add the following ingredients in this exact order: vetiver, bergamot, then bay leaves. Stir with the cinnamon stick.

Return the heat to low. Next add three blueberries, one for the bride, one for the groom, and one for the person presiding over the ceremony. After they have been added to the water, use the cinnamon stick to crush each one. Stir again.

Increase the heat. Finally, add the geranium, then the lavender, and then the peppermint. Stir periodically with the cinnamon stick for at least five minutes. Remove from heat. Let cool.

The spell should be cast while standing next to (or on) the road nearest to the wedding site. If performed during the day, face the sun. If performed at night, face the east, unless the wind is blowing, then put your back to the wind. Recite this spell:

> *Let all who wish us ill*
> *Travel the road at my feet*
> *Banish their thoughts*
> *Through this spell of defeat*

Repeat while pouring the potion onto the road.

WEDDING SACHET
JILL ROBI

Carry this sachet with you for good luck and positive energy on your wedding day. You will need:

- A red sachet
- Red, pink, and white rose petals
- Honeysuckle
- Head of 1 daisy
- Dried barley
- A sprinkle of vanilla
- A piece of gold

Take the sachet and bless it with this incantation, which you should repeat seven times: *Love freely, purely, and with passion.* Fill the sachet with the remaining ingredients. Say the incantation once more, sleep with the sachet under your pillow the night before the ceremony, and carry it on your special day.

TO KEEP A WIFE OR HUSBAND
TRADITIONAL

To attract and fix the affections of a mate, use this Cherokee shaman's charm: On your wedding night, when your new spouse is sleeping, take your saliva and rub it on your

SPELLS AND BLESSINGS FOR MARRIAGE AND ENGAGEMENTS

spouse's breast, reciting four times: *Your spittle, I take it, I eat it.*

Repeat this ceremony for three more nights, reciting four times on the second night: *Your body, I take it, I eat it.* And four times on the third night: *Your flesh, I take it, I eat it.*

And four times on the final night: *Your heart, I take it, I eat it.*

Then recite:

> *Listen! O, now you have drawn near to hearken, O, Ancient One. This woman's [or man's] soul has come to rest at the edge of your body. You are never to let go your hold upon it. It is ordained that you shall do just as you are requested to do. Let her never think upon any other place. Her soul has faded within her. She is bound by the black threads. This ceremony is so effective that no husband need have any fears for his wife after performing it.*

WEDDING NIGHT PASSION SPELL
DES D. WILSON

Light a white candle in the room where you will be spending your wedding night. Size doesn't matter—the candle can be big or small, tall or short—but it does need to be white in color, which signifies purity, peace, and true love. Before you begin, you and your partner should both imbibe about a shot-glass's worth of the following love potion, which you will have prepared no more than twenty-four hours in advance:

- 1 tablespoon extra-virgin palm oil (or, even better, 3–4 crushed or pureed palm seeds, also known as palm nuts or palm kernels)
- 2 tablespoons chopped and pounded arugula leaves
- ¼ cup organic sugar cane juice

As you drink, recite the following short incantation:

Spirits of Passion come tonight,
and stay here until morning light.
Fill my beloved with desire,
and stoke my love to roaring fire.

AFTER-WEDDING GOOD INTENTIONS RITUAL
ANASTASIA GREYWOLF

After the whirlwind of your wedding day, take some time to perform this ritual with your new spouse, which will help make your dreams come true and remember the joyous day of your union. Light pink and white candles and discuss with each other your favorite moments from

SPELLS AND BLESSINGS FOR MARRIAGE AND ENGAGEMENTS

your wedding, big and small. Take turns writing out these moments on pieces of paper. Then give the paper to your spouse, who will put it in an envelope and address the envelope to yourselves. For the address, write where you hope to live someday in the future, whether it's a modest dream you're actively working to obtain, a wild dream like traveling together abroad, or even something symbolic, like living together at the top of Mt. Everest. Switch off writing and addressing with each other. Then tie the letters with a red string and leave in a dresser, closet, or other space you two share. Open the letters whenever you'd like to read them, but make sure to make a circle (page 4) first and read them inside. It's also better to read them together than alone.

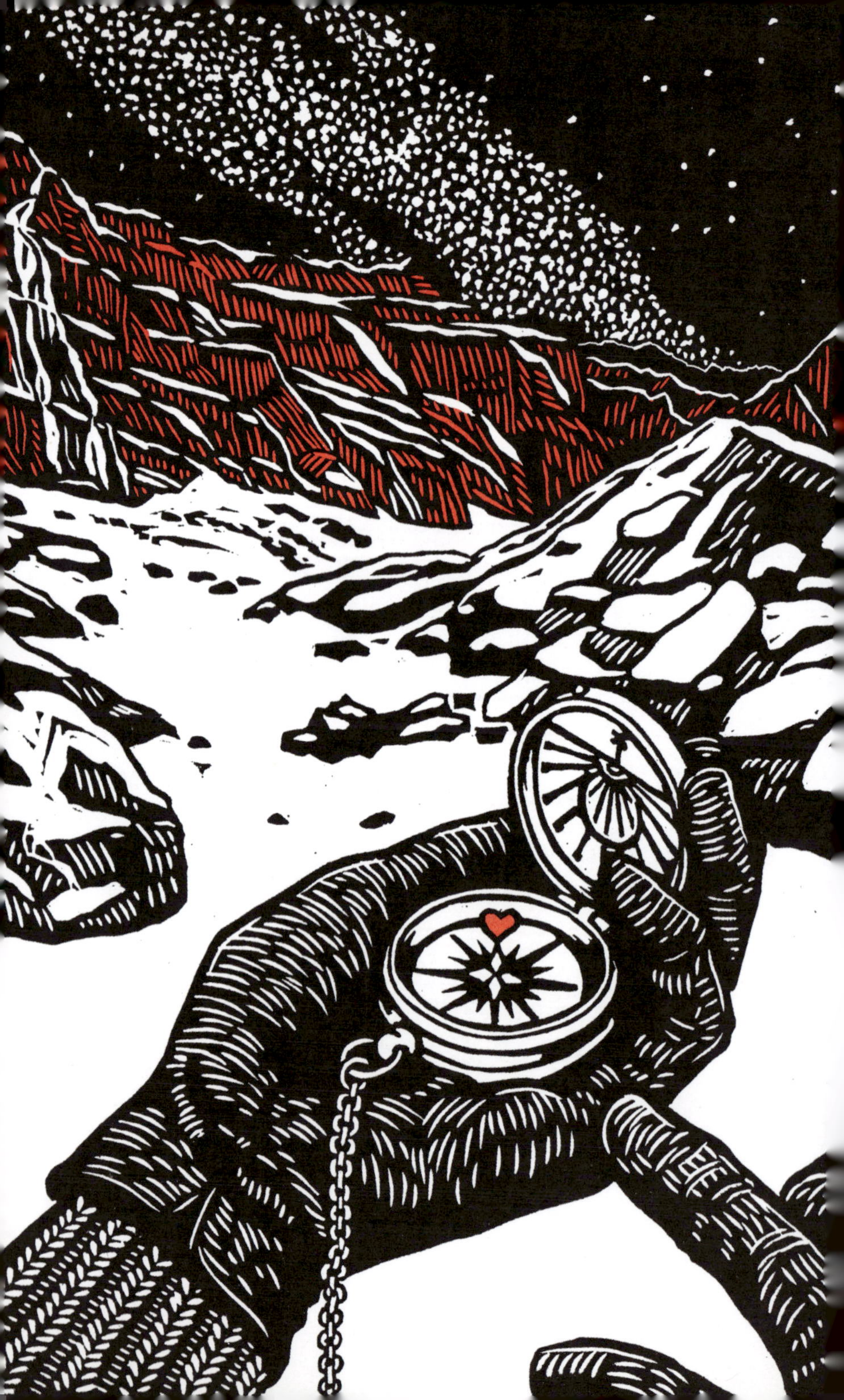

SPELLS AND POTIONS TO END A LOVE OR RELATIONSHIP

TO FORGET ABOUT PASSIONATE MEMORIES
JILL ROBI

On red paper anointed with almond oil, write down your strongest, most passionate memories in great detail. At the top of the page, write the name of the person who gave you the memories. Fold it and pick it up with tongs. Hold this over a white candle (place aluminum foil or a metal tray underneath for safety), keeping your thoughts pure. Chant *I am free, for my thoughts shall not take hold of me* as it burns to ash.

FOR COURAGE TO BREAK UP WITH YOUR LOVER
AOIFE WITT

A spell to get up the courage to break up with someone. (Important note: Most of us dread breaking up with a significant other. If the reason you are nervous about initiating a breakup is because your significant other may become violent, you may do this spell but please do not rely on it. Go to a safe place, and call the proper authorities.)

If you need courage to end a relationship, it may help to call on a power greater than yourself. Sit by yourself in a quiet place and breathe, deeply and smoothly, until you are centered. Then call the entity you feel closest to. It could be a deity, a spirit guide, familiar, an ancestor, or even the Earth itself. Whomever you call, make sure you trust this entity.

Explain why you have to end the relationship you're in. Envision in detail how much better your life will be when the relationship is over.

If you still need courage after this step, ask your guide to witness a memory of yourself being the bravest you've ever been. Now ask your deity to help you duplicate the courage from that first memory so that you can break up with your significant other. Ask them what they'd like as a gift in exchange for helping you. If you agree to the gift, write it down on a piece of paper. Carry it around as a charm until you complete your breakup. Once the breakup is over, leave the gift for your guide and burn the piece of paper.

To amplify this spell's power, wear an item of red clothing and perform it during the waning moon.

FREEZE OUT CHARM
TRADITIONAL

To get someone out of your life, obtain an object of theirs. Try for something they kept by them often, or even wore—like a ring, an item from their wallet, or sunglasses. Place it in a bowl of water (plastic works best), and let it freeze into a chunk of ice (place a lid on top if necessary to keep the item from floating to the top). As long as you keep the item suspended in the ice, the person will feel a chill toward you.

BREAKUP BATH
JILL ROBI

Take four pillar candles and light them for each corner of your bath. As the bath fills with warm water, place rosemary, lavender, and thyme in the bath. Hold Lemurian seed crystals between both palms, near to your heart, as you step into the bath. Focus on healing your heart, filling yourself with positive energy and letting go of the sadness and hurt. After a while, let the crystals drop into the water, letting them fuse with the special bath water. Once you finish with the bath, put the crystals into a sachet with fresh rosemary, lavender, and thyme, and keep close to you as a charm for a more restful sleep.

TO END A BAD DATE
SUSAN ADCOX

Whether you look for matches online or let your friends fix you up, sooner or later you're going to be trapped in a really bad date. Use this spell to bring the date to a speedy end. Since you may not have traditional spell ma-

SPELLS AND POTIONS TO END A LOVE OR RELATIONSHIP

terials at hand, you can improvise a banishing powder by mixing salt and pepper and scattering it as you repeat the spell. You can make a trip to the powder room or find a quiet corner to cast your spell. Of course, you could just walk out and hail a cab!

Let fate intervene!
Make conversation cease.
Make time take wing;
Let me have peace.

Make drink go dry,
Let dinner be downed,
And send me home
Safe, sane, and sound.

REVERSE LOVE SPELL
ANASTASIA GREYWOLF

If you believe you've been under a love spell and you no longer wish to be under it, this charm will reverse it. Obtain a stick from a tree the person has touched. Sharpen it. Use it to carve their name on the side of a white candle. Light the candle, and when it has burned out, bury it as far away from your home as possible.

LETTING GO OF LOVE
JILL ROBI

Take a photo of you and your former lover. Cut it right down the middle, separating them from you. Write on the back of the photo, *I release you, and in turn you release me*. Take the head of a dandelion, one that has opened and bloomed, and put that and the folded photo into a balloon. Fill the balloon with helium. On a Sunday, just before the sun rises, chant, *I release you, and in turn you release me*, as you let the balloon go. Keep chanting until the balloon is no longer in sight.

SPELLS AND POTIONS TO END A LOVE OR RELATIONSHIP

◆ TO LOSE ONE'S INFATUATION WITH AN ILLICIT LOVE
TRADITIONAL

If one has been infatuated by an illicit love, such a person must put a pair of shoes on and walk therein until their feet perspire; this person must walk fast, so that their feet do not smell badly. Then they must take off the right shoe, drink some beer or wine out of this shoe, and from that moment they shall lose all affection for the illicit lover.

FOR BANDAGING PAST WOUNDS
ANASTASIA GREYWOLF

If you have past emotional wounds that are holding you back from truly experiencing love, you can bandage them and get rid of them with this ritual. First, name the wounds by writing out the events that transpired to cause the injuries with black ink on white paper—use one slip of paper for each issue. You can write down specific instances in a relationship, overall injuries, or anything negative that's lingering psychically. Sit in a quiet place facing west and place the pieces of paper in a circle in front of you. Dip your finger in red paint and then put it on top of the paper closest to you. While your finger is on the paper, think about what's written on the paper and specifically the pain the event caused you. Or, if that is too much, simply acknowledge to yourself that what's on the paper did, indeed, cause a wound. Repeat the process for each paper in the circle, dipping your finger in fresh paint each time. Then take one more pass around the circle, this time picking up each paper and pressing it onto your body to leave a mark from the paint. Allow yourself to fully feel the negative feeling as you press the paper to your body, but try not to think about the event itself.

Finally, place a bandage over each wound, giving time and care to each as you would to a child. You may want to use larger bandages for larger wounds. As you bandage over each one, try to wipe your mind of all negative energy surrounding the incident. Wear the bandages until they fall off naturally.

TO PURGE ITEMS OF THEIR ASSOCIATION WITH AN EX
JOSEPHINE PRESTON PEABODY

If you own an item that you mentally associate with an ex-lover, and you would like to break the association, place the item in a black sachet or wrap it in a black cloth. Light some sage or sage incense and recite:

> *Yesterday has flown away*
> *Far beyond the sun.*
> *And of morrows, who can say,*
> *Till another one?*
> *Only Now is all my own,*
> *And my heart knows how:*
> *O wild wings for a sky unknown,*
> *Mine, mine—now!*

TO RELIEVE YOURSELF OF UNREQUITED LOVE
JILL ROBI

Run a warm bath with Epsom salts, and place black onyx stones in each corner of the tub. As you step into the water, chant, *Free from pain. Free from sorrow.* Continue the chant as you pour the water over yourself until it cools. For one week after the bath, carry an onyx stone with you (in your pocket, bag, or car) to keep the unrequited energy at bay.

TO EASE UNREQUITED LOVE
TRADITIONAL

To get over the pain of loving someone who doesn't love you in return, capture their reflection in a mirror (using a photo of them will work, although it's not as strong as their in-person reflection), then break the mirror while their reflection is in it. This charm is better performed with a friend, for safety. Clean up the shards yourself and bury them in the ground. You will feel the person's influence fading fast and will be free of the burden for seven years.

SPELLS AND POTIONS TO END A LOVE OR RELATIONSHIP

THE NARCISSA
HOLLEN POCKETS

This is a spell to fall in love with yourself. Perform in times of need.

Take a rock and break your mirrors. You don't need them right now.

Keep the rock and break your scales.

Take some scissors and snip your measuring tape.

Keep the scissors and cut your hair, no mirrors needed. Speak the words: *It doesn't matter. It will grow.*

Go for a long walk or get out of the house in whatever way you can. Use your body. Count the beats of your great heart.

Find a reflective pool. If needed, fill your favorite bathtub and look into that.

Speak the words: *I have all I need.*

Smile at your reflection, blurry and imperfect in the reflecting water. Smile and smile and smile.

UNBINDING/UNTANGLING SPELL
KATRIEL WINTERS

Here's a spell for when a relationship or acquaintance is bothering you and you wish to untangle your life from theirs. You might call it a "getting them out of your hair" spell. There are several versions of this: a classic version is tying two ropes together to represent the current situation and then untying them or ritually cutting them. A modern version might look like:

Take two paper clips or pieces of yarn, and mark one to symbolize youself with a piece of tape or other marker. Intertwine them. With paper clips, for example, you can bend them to link them to each other. The next day, proclaim, *I release you*, while undoing the clips or untying the yarn. If possible, do something cleansing like washing your hands and your feet or taking a bath after the spell.

Another variant is to braid and unbraid hair and then wash it with the intent of rinsing away the tightness and hold the relationship has on you in the water.

BURN AWAY LOVE RITUAL
ANASTASIA GREYWOLF

To burn away the connection to someone you no longer love, you will need:

1 black candle

Flowers

Peppermint oil

A thorn

A flat rock

Place the candle on the rock and light it near an open window. Place flowers around it. Put peppermint oil somewhere where you can smell it.

Using a thorn, scratch the name of the person you want to be released from into the candle, and write their name on a piece of paper. Burn the paper. Bury the candle, rock, and ashes far away from your home.

UNLOCKING CHARM
ANASTASIA GREYWOLF

To break your connection to a past lover, light one red candle and one black candle during a full moon. While tying a red ribbon around a key, recite:

> *I open my heart like a lock and key*
> *Waiting for my true love to find their way to me*
> *So mote it be*

Snuff out the candle and wear the ribbon and key around your neck (or keep it close by) until you meet a new love.

TO DETER UNWANTED LOVERS
SUSAN ADCOX

When someone is drawn to you but you do not feel an attraction, you want to gently discourage that person's affections. Burn some incense, choosing a scent that can be used for dual purposes: to gently repel the other person and to create a protective aura around yourself. Pine and sandalwood are considered protective because they have a robust scent and because they are derived from sturdy trees rather than from frailer plants. If you have a truly obsessive admirer, you will need stronger magic. Recite this spell:

The tide that entices, let it ebb.
Be released from attraction's web.
Do not pursue the elusive lover.
Go your way, to seek another.

TO GET SOMEONE TO STOP TEXTING OR CALLING YOU
GABRIEL GREY

If someone is continually bothering you via phone call or text message, write their phone number on a piece of paper and place it on the ground. Burn the paper with a match with a red tip. Don't touch the ashes, and put dirt on them immediately to bury them.

TO MAKE A MAN LOSE HIS ROMANTIC VITALITY
TRADITIONAL

A mirror constructed in the following way can be used to great effect on your enemies: Take a mirror in a wooden frame and put it into a tub of water, so that it will float on the top with its face directed toward the sky. On the top of the mirror and encircling the glass, lay a wreath, and thus expose it to the influence of the new moon. This evil influence is thrown toward the moon, and radiating again from the moon it may bring evil to those who have to look upon it.

The rays of the moon passing through that ring upon the mirror become poisoned and poison the mirror; the mirror throws back ether to the atmosphere, and the moon and mirror poison each other in the same manner as two malicious persons looking at each other poison each other's souls with their eyes.

If a mirror is strongly poisoned in this manner, and the witch takes good care of it; and if she desires to injure someone, she may take a waxen image made in his name, surround it with a cloth spotted with menstrual blood, and throw the reflection of the mirror onto the figure, using at the same time her evil imagination and curses. The man whom the image represents may then have his vitality dried up.

TO MAKE AN EX GO AWAY
TRADITIONAL

To make an ex-lover go away, never to return, obtain a toad as well as some of the hairs from your ex's left leg. Tie the hairs to the left leg of the toad, and take the toad far away from where you found it (and far away from your own home). Set the toad free. Your ex will feel the desire to travel far away. Just be warned: This charm can be dangerous for your ex if the frog is harmed or eaten.

TO CURSE AN EX USING SALT AND PEPPER
TRADITIONAL

To curse an ex-lover who did you wrong, take salt and pepper and put it into their clothing, or in their house, and say:

> *I put this pepper on you,*
> *And this salt thereto,*
> *That peace and happiness*
> *You never more may know.*

TO GET RID OF STALKERS
ELISIA G

Stalkers are vampires who latch onto your energy. Sometimes they stalk you in obvious ways: through social media or by showing up at your work or other places where you are easy to find. At other times, the stalking is subtler; they "happen" to appear where you are as if by coincidence. The subtlest version of all is when everything on your path "mysteriously" reminds you of them: you meet a stranger with their name, etc.

Whether they stalk you by sniffing you out on the astral plane or by snooping around your Instagram, stalkers need to—and can be—dealt with in an efficient manner that protects your energy so that they can't get into your zone.

Start with a quiet space where you won't be interrupted. Turn off your phone. Close your eyes and breathe deeply. Once you're in a meditative space, imagine a red cord attached to your crown chakra that draws downward, tethering you to the earth. Feel how the red cord anchors you. Focus on your breath, and feel how this red cord pushes out energies that aren't yours and returns your energy to you.

Make a list of all the ways that the person stalks you. At the bottom write, *I am closing myself off to energies that are not mine. I am taking back my power. I am shutting the door to*

SPELLS AND POTIONS TO END A LOVE OR RELATIONSHIP

[name of person]. Put that list and everything that reminds you of that person in a bag. Cover the bag in perfume to throw them off your scent. Afterward, keep your phone off, stay off social media, and don't go to any of your usual haunts for as long as possible. If possible, stay out of your usual routine for a whole twenty-four hours in order to reset your cycle.

Accompanying Tarot cards for your altar: Seven of Cups reversed, the Hermit.

TO HEAL ANGER AT A LOST LOVER
DES D. WILSON

Anger consumes and destroys. It is, of course, natural to feel angry sometimes, but understand that whenever you are angry, your rational and spiritual self is blocked. You are not thinking clearly and thus you cannot be your best self. This powerful spell will help you heal any anger you may be feeling over a lost lover.

Sit quietly for a few minutes in a pleasant and comfortable spot—outdoors or indoors, it doesn't matter, as long as you personally find it nice and comfortable. The beach, a beautiful garden, or just your bedroom—really, anything will do. Now focus on your breath. If thoughts or feelings start to intrude, try not to get frustrated, but also don't get caught up in these thoughts and feelings; gently direct your awareness back to your breath.

Once you're feeling quite settled, light a white candle on an elevated surface, such as a table or desk. The candle must be white, since white represents purity, peace, and true love. Before the candle and on the same surface, place three small quartz stones, a bowl of clean water, a bowl containing pure extra-virgin palm oil, and a freshly cut pink or white rose. Gazing fixedly at the spot just above the tip of the flame, recite the following words five times in succession, in a neutral and unemotional tone of voice:

> *I'm freeing my mind and healing my heart;*
> *in my rediscovery, anger and rancor play no part.*
> *Fury be gone, the past is done; I'm starting over.*

TO BANISH YOUR ENEMY
TRADITIONAL

To banish your enemy, collect dirt from their shoes or clothing. Mix it with cayenne pepper, then grind it with sassafras and coffee grounds, preferably those used to make coffee your enemy drank. Sprinkle the mixture in front of your enemy's door and that person will leave your community.

FOR BANISHING SOMEONE WITH FOUR THIEVES' VINEGAR
TRADITIONAL

To banish someone, mix the potion known as four thieves' vinegar. Combine together apple cider vinegar, rosemary, sage, lavender, wormwood, and camphor. Place the concoction in a jar in a dark corner for two months before opening. Then apply to the doorknob of the person you wish to banish.

FREEDOM FIRE SPELL
ANASTASIA GREYWOLF

If you want to get your freedom back, or have recently received some freedom that you weren't welcoming, say this spell while staring into a fire to gain strength. For even better results, burn some sage in the fire to cleanse yourself of bad associations.

> *Fire, fire, toil and trouble*
> *Release me from this self-made bubble*
> *I'm free, aloft, like a bat in the night*
> *Gonna find my inner fire, I know I have a light*
> *Because in the spirit forest*
> *Away from men and noise*
> *There's something deep inside me*

Approaching ageless poise
It doesn't need wisdom to know what to do
It doesn't even need love, or anything new
Because it's never changed, it was there from day one
That freedom fire, every battle to be won
So bring it forth among the melee
Trust it to lead us forward
Wherever the way
The freedom fire, it's there in me
To let it burn
Simply just be

TO RID YOURSELF OF YOUR EX'S TOXIC ENERGY
DES D. WILSON

They say that time heals all wounds, and indeed, normally an ex's toxic and harmful energy will go away by itself after a while. But sometimes their energy lingers on for too long, and stronger measures are needed. This magic will

SPELLS AND POTIONS TO END A LOVE OR RELATIONSHIP

help you get rid of this noxious influence. Before casting the spell, though, make sure you have disposed of any items belonging to your ex, except those that are strictly necessary for practical or legal reasons. Unfortunately, material things can retain some of the energy of their owner, and depending of the amount of energy stored in the item, your ex's possessions could undermine the spell's power or even nullify it. For this reason, it is very important not to have your ex's stuff lying around when saying the spell. Light a tall blue candle, placing it on an elevated surface such as a table, desk, or stool. Set before the candle a bowl of clean water, three heads of garlic, a blue gemstone (such as agate, aquamarine or lapis lazuli), and a large green palm leaf. The palm leaf will transform into a shield protecting you against your ex's bad energy, as well as any spirits that may be supporting your ex. With a calm mind and a neutral tone of voice, utter the following incantation five times:

> *All negative energies and presences are banished from this space.*
> *Poisonous impressions, depart! Only love resides in this place.*
> *I am shielded and safe; I move on, I heal, and I grow.*

FOR CURING HEARTBREAK
DY EDWARDS

Use this spell to acknowledge the pain of lost or betrayed love and move on from it. When performed correctly, the magician should be able to find peace again.

You will need:
Water
A bottle that was full of something they gave you
    (or a box, a cup, a scrap of a scarf)
Dried thistle
A compass
A stout pocketknife
A mug and a tea bag
Good boots
A candle is nice, but never necessary,
But a lantern is good sense
Do not bring your favorite flower,
Or wear anything they loved you in
(The memories will follow you).

Take the bottle and bury it as far away from you
    as you can get,
(But never in the sea—
The sea rolls back and they will find you again).
Crush the thistle in your hands.
It will stab you, but that's okay.
Blow away the dust;
The pain will fade if you let it.

SPELLS AND POTIONS TO END A LOVE OR RELATIONSHIP

✦ ✦ ✦

Take a long walk and a deep breath.
Keep the compass in your pocket.
Find a mountain,
Or a forest,
And walk.
Drink the water when you need it;
Use the compass if you feel lost.
If you meet someone who needs directions,
Or water,
Or company,
Help them. Ask for nothing in return.
If they offer you sugar, or honey, you can take it.
Do not leave them where you found them,
But don't stay with them either.

When your boots come untied and your feet hurt,
Stop and look around.
This might be where they left your heart.
If you can, make camp.
The knife will help you cut tinder.
Look up at the sky;
There should be stars if we did this right.
Boil your water.
If you have sugar or honey, put it in the mug.
Then the tea bag.
When the water is boiled, pour it in.
Mix. Steep. Wait.

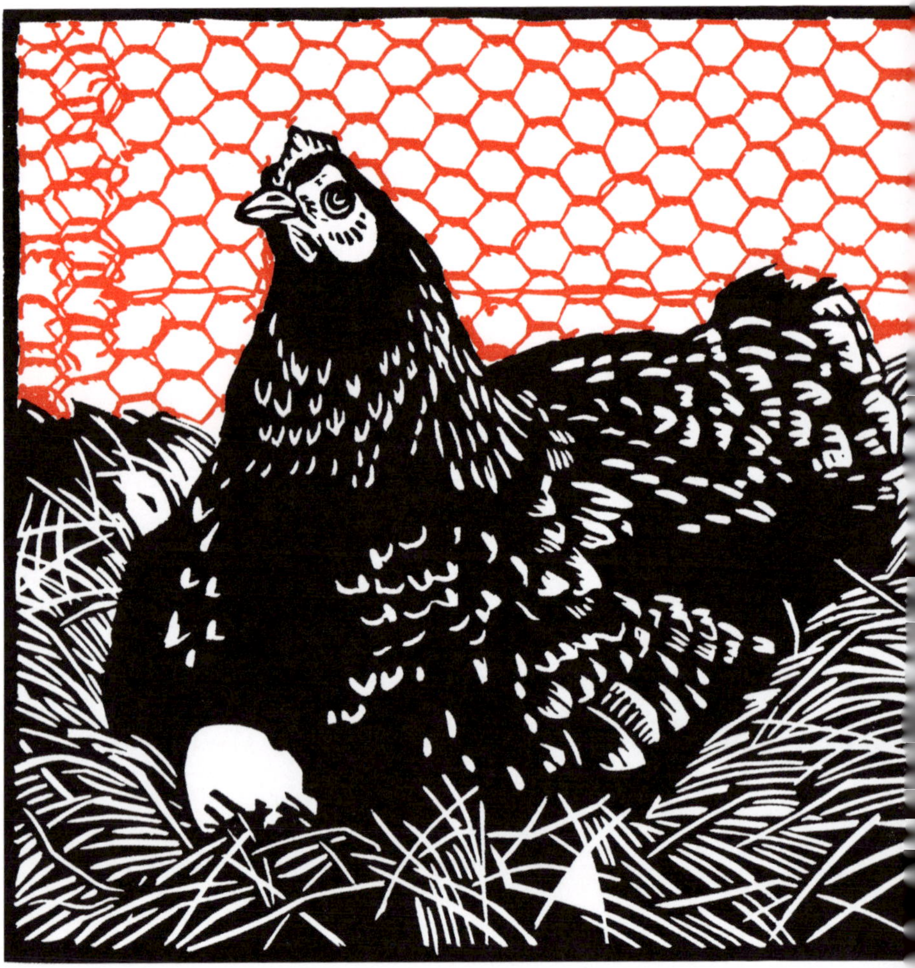

LISTS OF SYMBOLS AND OMENS

◆ Love Omens

APPLES

Apples are a lucky sign in love and are good to use in spells. If you press apple seeds against your forehead, the number that stick is the number of days until you see your beloved. You can also twist an apple stem, reciting the alphabet, and the letter the stem breaks on is the first letter of name of the person you will marry.

APRONS

If you wipe your hand on someone's apron, they will fall in love with you. It's also said that if your apron falls off, that means your beloved is thinking of you.

BIRTHDAYS

Don't marry on your (or your future spouse's) birthday, as the person whose birthday it is may die an early death.

BOBBY PINS

If you have a bobby pin in your hair and it falls out, you will lose your beloved.

BREAD CRUST

Carrying a crust of bread in one's pocket is considered lucky and brings prosperity.

BRIDAL BEDS

It is considered lucky for girls to sit on a bride's bed, as it will cause other marriages.

BRIDESMAIDS

You should never be a bridesmaid more than twice, or you will never be married yourself.

BRIDGES

It's bad luck to say goodbye to your love at a bridge. If you part at a bridge, you will part forever.

BROTHERS

It is unlucky for three married brothers to live in the same town.

CABBAGE

If you pull a cabbage out of the earth and it has a straight root, you will marry someone attractive, but if it has a crooked root, he will not be. If the cabbage is very dirty, you will marry someone wealthy.

CANDLES

Keep a candle burning in your front window while your love is away and they will always return.

CATS

If you see a strange cat near your home, that means your lover is faithful to you. If you see a cat sneezing on your wedding day, that is also a good omen.

CIGARS

If you take a puff of someone else's cigar, you will fall in love with the next person who enters the room.

CLOTHING, BACKWARDS

If you accidentally put an article of clothing on backwards while dressing, it's a good omen for your relationship.

CLOVER

If you find a two-leaf clover, place it in your shoe. The first person who approaches you from the side of that shoe will someday marry you.

COMBS

If you drop your comb, you'll see your beloved before you need to comb your hair again. But never let them carry your comb, or you will lose their heart to someone else.

DOGS

If someone loves dogs, that is a sign they will be a good spouse.

DREAMS

If you dream about someone, it's an omen that they went to sleep thinking about you. If you dream of taking a bath, it's an omen that you'll fall in love soon.

EATING

If you always leave food on your plate after eating, you will marry someone unattractive.

ELBOWS

If you keep your elbows dirty, you will marry someone without many future prospects.

FEET

If you accidentally step on your lover's foot, they must step on your foot as well or you will soon get into an argument.

FIRE

If you make a fire that burns well, it means your lover has a fiery passion for you. If it goes out, it means your lover's passion is starting to wane.

KETTLES

If your teakettle sings, it is a sign of happiness and contentment in your home. If you are single, don't allow a kettle to point toward the wall. If it boils, you will never marry.

HAIRY LEGS

Women with hairy legs are said to be more likely to find love.

HANDKERCHIEFS

If you give someone a handkerchief as a gift, you will never be married.

HICCUPS

If you think of your lover when you have the hiccups and the hiccups stop, that means they love you.

HORSES, WHITE

If you see two white horses on a bridge, make a wish that you will get married and it will come true.

KNIVES

Don't get your beloved a knife as a present, as it means your relationship will soon be severed.

LADDERS

If you walk under an open ladder, you won't find a mate for another year.

LADYBUGS

If a ladybug lands on you, let it go and it will fly toward the direction of your future mate.

LIPS, ITCHY

If your lips are itching, that means you'll kiss someone soon.

LOVE MESSAGES

If you receive a love message from two different people on the same day, you will marry neither of them.

MANURE

For good luck and prosperity in your home, surround it with manure.

MIRRORS

Never place a mirror next to your bed, or you'll begin to have uncontrollable sexual urges.

MOLES

If you find a mole (the animal), and strike it on its right foot, and it will bring you true love.

MYRTLE TREES

Myrtle trees are considered extremely lucky for love.

NECKLACES

If your necklace clasp rotates to the front of your body so it's over your throat, that means someone is thinking of you fondly.

NEW YEAR'S EVE

If you are in a relationship, it's bad luck not to kiss your beloved at midnight on New Year's.

NOSE, ITCHY

If your nose itches, you have a secret admirer somewhere.

ONIONS

If you eat onions on Saturday night, then you won't see your sweetheart the next day.

PENCILS

Never write a love letter in pencil, or the love won't last.

POPPY SEEDS

If you strike a poppy seed and it makes a popping noise, your lover is faithful to you.

POTS

If you drop a pot and it lands upside down, you will soon see someone you love again.

PROPOSALS

If someone turns down a proposal that was made at a public function, they will have good luck in love for the rest of their life.

RABBITS

If you see several rabbits in your yard, it's a sign that you are fertile and may get pregnant soon.

RAIN

If it rains on your wedding day, that's a good omen for your marriage.

RICE

Throw rice on the bride and groom after a wedding to bring them health, prosperity, and happiness.

RINGS, ENGAGEMENT

Never try on someone else's engagement ring on your left hand if you're unmarried or you will never marry yourself.

RINGS, WEDDING

If a bride or groom drops a wedding ring during the ceremony, they will be the first spouse to die.

SAND DOLLARS

If you're walking on the beach with your love and find a sand dollar, you will be together forever.

SCISSORS

If you drop scissors, it is an omen that your lover might be unfaithful to you.

SHOOTING STARS

If you observe a shooting star while with your beloved, make a wish about your relationship and it will come true.

SKIRTS

If the corner of your skirt turns up, your lover is at a bar.

SNEEZING

If you sneeze before breakfast, you'll see your sweetheart before the day is through. Sneezing at the same time as your beloved is a sign you will have good fortune.

SPIDERS

Seeing a spider on a date or your wedding day is a good omen.

SPIDER WEBS

Although spiders may be good luck, spider webs are not. If you see a spider web in your bedroom, that portends bad luck for your love life.

SPOONS

If you eat from the same spoon as your spouse, it will cause fighting in your relationship.

STAIRS

If you stumble while trying to go up stairs, you will soon find love.

SWEEPING

Don't let someone sweep over your feet, or you will never marry.

TABLES

Never sit at the corner of a table; it will be bad for your love life.

TOADS

If a toad crosses your path, you will soon meet a true love.

TOASTING

When clinking glasses during a toast, it's important to look the person you're toasting with in the eyes, or you will be cursed with seven years of bad sex.

TOWELS

It's bad luck for two lovers to dry off with the same towel. It portends that they will soon argue and even break up.

TWITCHING

If you find your right side twitching, that means your lover is thinking of you.

VEILS

Wear a veil on your wedding day to ward off evil spirits.

WEDDING, BEFORE

For a bride and groom to see each other on the day of the wedding before the ceremony is bad luck.

WEDDING CAKE

Save your wedding cake for one year, then eat it together as a couple for good luck.

WEDDING DRESS

For good luck, don't complete the final stitch of a wedding dress until the bride is departing for the wedding, which fools evil spirits into thinking the wedding isn't soon.

WINE, SPILLING

To spill wine while drinking a toast is a good omen and brings health and happiness to the person who spilled it.

WISHBONES

If two people break a wishbone together, the one who gets the shorter piece will marry sooner than the one who gets the longer piece. "Shortest to marry, longest to tarry."

Love Birds

Birds have been associated with love throughout the ages and in many cultures. Here are some of the omens regarding birds that can affect your love life.

BLUEBIRDS

Bluebirds will bring happiness in your relationship.

CARDINALS

If you see a cardinal on your wedding day, make a wish for your marriage and it will come true.

CHICKENS

On midnight on Christmas Eve night, knock on a chicken coop. If the chickens cackle, you will find love during that year. If not, you won't. Additionally, if an all-black hen that has never laid an egg before lays an egg on Thursday, bury it and love will come to you.

CROWS

Seeing crows or other black birds near your home means that it will be protected.

CUCKOOS

If you hear a cuckoo bird at the beginning of spring, count how many times it coos and that's how many years you will be married.

DOVES

Seeing a dove is a good omen for long-lasting love.

DUCKS

See two ducks together and you will soon find a new love.

EAGLES

If you and your beloved see an eagle together early in your relationship, it is a sign the relationship will go well.

GEESE

If you see your lover with a goose, be aware that he may surprise you with bad news or not have your best interests at heart.

OWLS
Seeing an owl with your beloved can be a bad sign for your relationship.

PEACOCKS
Peacocks represent strength and can bring you luck in finding love.

ROBINS
If you see a robin fly over your head on Valentine's Day, you will marry a sailor.

ROOSTERS
If a rooster crows at your back door, it is a sign that someone in the house will die.

SWALLOWS
Seeing a swallow with your partner means a period of rebirth for your relationship is coming soon.

SWANS
Swans symbolize long-lasting love and marriage.

Moon Phases and Love Magic

The moon is a powerful force, and what kind of moon you perform love spells under can impact the way the spells affect you or others. Here is what you need to know about each phase of the moon as it relates to love magic.

NEW MOON

Understandably, a new moon is perfect for spells that call for a new beginning. It's also good for fertility spells.

WAXING MOON

A waxing moon is a moon that's starting to become a full moon. It's especially good for passion spells and spells to find a lover.

FULL MOON

A full moon is the best time to perform most spells, including love spells. Because it is fully exposed, you can take advantage of its full energy. It also helps turn negative energy into positive energy. It's said that the seventh day after a full moon is the most ideal time for two people to fall in love at first sight.

WANING MOON

A waning moon is the moon that's displayed after a full moon, when it is moving back into its crescent shape. A waning moon keeps away negative spirits and influences, so if you are performing a fidelity spell or another spell to ward off evil, this is the best time to do it.

🍀 Lucky Days for Love

Some days of the year are better spiritually than others. Here are some days that are known to be auspicious for love, and are especially good days to perform love spells.

JANUARY
1, 2, 15, 26, 27, 28

FEBRUARY
11, 21, 25, 26

MARCH
10, 24

APRIL
6, 15, 16, 20, 28

MAY
3, 13, 18, 31

JUNE
10, 11, 15, 22, 25

JULY
9, 14, 15, 18

AUGUST

6, 7, 10, 11, 19, 20, 25

SEPTEMBER

4, 8, 9, 17, 18, 23

OCTOBER

3, 7, 16, 21, 22

NOVEMBER

5, 14, 20

DECEMBER

14, 15, 19, 20, 22, 23, 25

Love Stones

Various stones give off different energies. Here are some that are good to use in your love charms.

AMBER

If you want to receive a marriage proposal, try carrying or working with amber.

AMETHYSTS

Amethysts promote harmony and are good to work with to protect and heal from arguments.

LOVE MAGIC

CAT'S EYE
Cat's eye is known to strengthen your inner self; it's great for when you are trying to find love or stay strong for a loved one.

CITRINE
Citrine is a good stone to carry on you at any time, because it increases the efficacy of spells and works almost as a purifier, keeping neutral energy all around it.

EMERALDS
Emeralds can help bring you the support you need in tough times. They also help build loyalty in relationships.

DIAMONDS
Diamonds symbolize a deepening of trust and commitment, as well as a bright future.

GARNETS
A great stone for passion, garnet can increase your sex drive and romantic love.

JADE
Jade promotes a long-lasting relationship and is also beneficial when rebuilding trust between two loved ones.

MOONSTONES
In some traditions, moonstone is thought to attract love.

PEARLS
Pearls can bring about a beautiful love.

PINK SAPPHIRES

If you're looking for a new love, wear or work with pink sapphires.

RHODONITE

Rhodonite brings happiness and helps prevent loneliness.

ROSE QUARTZ

Rose quartz may be one of the best love stones. It not only represents romantic love, but love and compassion for yourself.

RUBIES

Rubies are a useful stone for regaining a lost love. They are also a good fertility stone.

TIGER'S EYE

Tiger eye helps you focus on your third eye and can bring you courage and power.

TOPAZ

Topaz brings honesty and tenderness, and is good for friendships.

TURQUOISE

Turquoise a plentiful yet bright and beautiful stone that is good for friendship spells.

🔲 Love Colors

Colors have special meaning in witchcraft and spell-casting. Here are the associations and spirits represented by various colors.

BLACK

Work with black to get rid of negativity or negative associations.

BLUE

Blue is a good color for ensuring fidelity and willpower.

GOLD

If you want a love that lasts, gold is a great color for representing durability.

GREEN

Green represents prosperity in a relationship and in life. Green can also symbolize the earth and all of the living things it contains (including your loves).

ORANGE

Display or work with orange objects to bring about happiness and good communication in a relationship.

PINK

Pink represents friendship, compassion, and harmony and is also a good color when healing from a fight.

PURPLE

Purple is the color of purity and can also signal spiritual strength and healing.

RED

Desire, vitality, and passion all come forth when red is displayed.

WHITE

White is a good color for new beginnings.

YELLOW

Yellow can represent completeness. It is also the color of friendliness.

Love Flowers

Flowers are a symbol of affection when given to someone you love, but some flowers are better than others. Here are the specific meanings of various flowers.

ARTIFICIAL FLOWERS

Having a home with only artificial flowers can be bad luck in terms of filling it with love.

AMBROSIA

Seeing or receiving ambrosia means your beloved loves you back.

ASTERS

Working with asters can help you find love.

AZALEAS

Azaleas are a good flower to use when performing passion spells.

BABY'S BREATH

Baby's breath symbolizes purity of heart and soul and can be useful when trying to attract the right kind of mate.

BOUQUETS

Throw your wedding bouquet after your wedding and the first person who catches it will be the next person to get married.

CARNATIONS

Carnations are often used in love spells, and different colors can mean different things. While yellow carnations can mean disappointment or rejection, white carnations in spells can lead to finding someone sweet and kind. Pink carnations represent motherly or familial love, while red carnations represent passion.

DAISIES

If you pick a clump of daisies with your eyes closed, the number of daisies you pick will be the number of years you must wait until you're married.

DANDELIONS

If you find a dandelion puff, blow on it. The number of times you have to blow for all of the seeds to fly away is the number of years you must wait to be married.

LAVENDER

Use lavender to increase faithfulness and devotion.

LILACS

Lilacs can be bad luck if you give them to your beloved.

MARIGOLDS

Seeing marigolds is a good omen for long-lasting love.

PANSIES

Pansies are bad luck and should not be picked early in the morning, or your lover will die.

PRIMROSE

Use primrose to effect everlasting love.

ROSES

Because of both their beauty and their thorns, roses are good flowers to represent love when performing spells and charms. Red roses represent true love.

YELLOW FLOWERS

If someone gives you yellow flowers, it's a sign they may have betrayed you and you should be suspicious.

Note on drying flowers: Try tying the stems of the flowers to a clothes hanger so that the blooms hang down. Hang it on a wall or door for about a week. For quicker results, pick up some silica gel at the craft store; it dries out flowers in two to three days. —Greta Goldbart

Love Herbs and Spices

Use these herbs and spices in your love magic to get the results you need. You can burn them, eat them, make a tea by infusing hot water with them, or just leave them nearby to inhale their scent as you perform your spell.

BASIL

Basil promotes fidelity, loyalty, and true love. It can also bring luck and happiness.

BAY LEAVES

A traditional symbol of two partners coming together, can also indicate prosperity and good fortune.

CATNIP

Unsurprisingly, catnip is a potent herb for use in cat love and friendship spells.

CAYENNE PEPPER

Use cayenne or any chili pepper if you want passion and spiciness in your relationship.

CLOVES

Cloves drive away negative forces.

CINNAMON

Cinnamon is an all-purpose spice that can be used to increase any spell's efficacy.

DILL

Dill will protect you and your relationship from harm.

GINGER

Ginger can bring excitement into a relationship that needs it.

MARJORAM

Marjoram is beneficial for making sure the happiness of new relationships lasts or that life transitions are smooth.

MINT

Mint is good for healing and protecting against hexes from other witches.

NUTMEG

Nutmeg promotes success, especially financial prosperity and harmony for a couple.

PARSLEY

Parsley attracts good fortune and prosperity.

ROSEMARY

Rosemary is a traditional love and friendship herb that can also relate to memory.

SAFFRON

Saffron indicates romantic love and even lust.

SAGE

Sage has cleansing properties and is good for clearing negative energy and beginning a new slate.

SALT

Salt can represent the earth, but is also useful for when you need to create a barrier.

THYME

Thyme is beneficial for increasing courage and your ability to get someone's attention.

VANILLA

Vanilla can be used to bring joy or sensuality into one's life.

Essential Oils Used in Love Magic

Anointing yourself or sacred objects with oil can be an important ritual. Use these essential oils to guide your magic-making. You can also burn incense in these scents.

BERGAMOT

Bergamot brings an undertone of happiness to any spell.

CEDAR

Cedar oil is good for protection and prosperity spells.

JASMINE

One of the best essential oils for love, jasmine is an overall love and harmony oil. It can also add to your sexuality, sensuality, and ability to seduce others.

LEMON

Lemon will bring a sense of new beginnings and joy into your life.

ORANGE

Orange oil is good for hope and optimism.

PATCHOULI

Patchouli symbolizes passion and a deep connection. It is also the oil of success, and is good to use before a date.

SAGE

Sage is good for cleansing negative energy and establishing a neutral space for spellwork to occur.

SANDALWOOD

If you're trying to see the future of your lovelife, sandalwood can help tap into a higher power to facilitate that.

ROSE

Rose is a good oil for attracting pure love and friendship.

YLANG YLANG

Ylang ylang will make love to come to you, and will also make you feel more sensual.

Contributors

Illustrator **Melissa West** is a painter and printmaker whose work explores the magical place where comfort and menace meet. She lives in Santa Cruz, California, and has exhibited in many galleries in the area as well as being featured in *Pilgrimage* magazine. You can see more of her artwork at MSWest.com and on Instagram at @mswest.art.

Susan Adcox, the author of *Stories From My Grandparent*, is a writer specializing in generational issues. She believes in many sources of spiritual strength and calls coastal Texas home.

Gemma Aronson is a creative copywriter from London who's written for *Fodors*, BuzzFeed, and others. She draws magical inspiration from nature and old ancient wiccan spells.

Jennifer Boudinot is a semi-practicing witch who writes about cocktails, including the books *Dangerous Cocktails* and the forthcoming *Viva Mezcal*.

DY Edwards is a kitchen witch and writer who lives in Michigan and talks far too much about her cat. To see more of her work, check out DYEdwards.com.

Elisia G. is one half of Ancient Nouveau, a cosmic collaboration of two old mystical warrior souls reunited in this lifetime to continue their karmic journey together of cultivating a potent spiritual community on Earth. As a renowned tarot card reader and Feng-Shui wizard, Mary's Brooklyn-based practice includes regular workshops on Tarot and spell-writing, as well as private readings for clients across the country. You can follow her on Instagram at @ancient.nouveau.

Greta Goldbart is an oracle who divines otherworldly secrets from beyond the veil. She's from Atlanta, Georgia, and is the proud mother of three snakes and a frog. Her favorite fabric is velvet.

Gabriel Grey is an urban warlock and musician with an interest in color, crystals, and other magic.

Anastasia Greywolf is a witch with an interest in all beliefs, spirits and spiritualities, gods, and traditions. She studies history and is the editor of *Witchcraft: A Handbook of Magic, Spells, and Potions*. She lives in the Northeastern United States with her two cats (one black, one fluffy) and is a founding member of the Coven of the Moonbeam Ravine.

CONTRIBUTORS

James Benjamin Kenyon is the author of *Harvest Home*, which was published in 1920.

Suzanne Lareau is a writer and editor who is drawn to affirmative spells and healing practices. In addition to her own writing, she works with authors to craft their message and shape their manuscripts. Lareau lives in the Washington Heights neighborhood of New York City, where an array of minority religions flourish and practitioners make creative use of city parks and the varied elements at hand.

Savana Lee is a writer, mom, and yogi from Colorado. She has been featured in Elephant Journal, Every Day Fiction, and is currently finishing her first magical novel. When she's not writing you can find her with her family, painting, or reading.

Josephine Preston Peabody lived during the turn of the twentieth century in Brooklyn, New York, and Dorchester, Massachusetts. She is the author of *The Singing Leaves: A Book of Songs and Spells*.

Hollen Pockets wasn't born into magic, but came into their powers through practice and determination. Hollen is in the Melbourne (Australia) coven and communicates with mortals on Twitter as @faceoddity.

Calyx Reed is a writer living in Portland, Oregon. You can find more of her work at CalyxReed.com.

Jill Robi is a writer, speaker, and film journalist from Chicago. The writer of Diary of a Fangirl (JillRobisFangirl.us), she is a movie aficionado, self-proclaimed geek, avid comic-con attendee, panelist, and cosplayer.

Elisa Shoenberger is a Chicago-based writer who believes the world is a temple. She has written for the Center for Humans and Nature's City Creatures site, Love TV, Sonderers, and the Reset. She is a regular contributor of Book Riot. She writes the travel and art blog Not Without My Bowler Hat and oral history project It Will Keep Your Heart Alive. She's also the co-editor and co-founder of The Antelope Magazine.

Jeanne de la Ware lives on an island in a tidal strait.

Marguerite Wilkinson was a poet and the author of *In Vivid Gardens*. She passed away in 1928.

Des D. Wilson is a funky warlock with a special interest in gemstones and protection spells. His magic comes from a variety of sources, but is particularly shaped by Afro-Caribbean and Sami traditions.

Katriel Winter is a mainly urban witch who melds nature-based ways with the contemporary realities of living. She specializes in candle magic and everyday nudges and lives on the Eastern Seaboard.

INDEX

Advice, giving, 29–30
Answers, finding, about partner, 103
Anxiety, easing, 34, 55, 86–87
Aphrodisiacs, 124
Apps, dating, 87
Attraction
 increasing, 120
 ending, 194, 197, 198, 202–203
Attractiveness, increasing, 59
Autumn, finding love in, 76–78
Babies, 161, 162–163. *See also* Fertility
Birds, talking to, 50
Breaking up, 105–106, 109, 186–209
 courage to, 186–187
 knowing if you should, 105–106, 109
 preventing, 143–144
 See also Exes
Cats, 41–42, 43–45, 46. *See also* Pets
Cheating. *See* Unfaithfulness
Commitment, fear of, 89
Counterspells, 60, 190
Coworkers, 70

Crushes
 contact from, 67–68
 coworkers, 70
 ending, 191, 194
Dating, 54, 55, 56, 69–70, 80–89
 Apps, 87
 Bad dates, ending, 188–189
 Blind dates, 84
 Confidence for, 55–56
 Commitment, 89
 First dates, 82, 83
 Good luck with, 85, 88
Desire. *See* Attraction
Dogs, 41–42. *See also* Pets
Dreaming, 66, 99, 118
Emails, 115–116. *See also* Love letters
Engagements. *See* Marriage, proposals
Exes
 cursing, 201
 getting over, 187, 188, 190, 191, 192, 193, 196–197, 198, 205–206, 206–207
 making go away, 200–201, 204, 205

Exes (cont.)
　reconciling with, 153, 154–155, 156. See also Breaking up
Eye contact, making, 69–70
Family, protecting, 163
Fertility, 158, 159–161
Fights
　after, cleansing, 152
　preventing, 30, 150–151
Flaws
　your lover's, 104–105
　our own, 126–127
Foreign languages, understanding, 64
Foreign places
　finding love from, 62–63
　making friends in, 15
Forgiveness, 33, 36
Freedom, 205–206
Freeze out charm, 187
Friends, 12–39
　communication with, 37–39
　conflicts with, minimizing, 28, 29, 30–31, 36
　female, 13
　finding, 12, 16–17, 18, 19–20
　forgiving, 33, 36
　long-distance, 14–15
　new, 22–23
　reconnecting with, 12, 13, 32–33
　romantic feelings for, 25, 26, 27
　tensions between, easing, 35
　while traveling, 15
Future partners
　arrival, time of, 106
　dreaming of, 99
　finding, 56, 57, 58, 69, 70
　first initial of, 103
　hair color of, 96–98,
　marriage of, 96, 98–99, 100, 166
　number of, 92
　pure, 71–73
　qualities in 58, 69
　seeing, 92, 93–94, 106
Gossip, ending, 28
Healing, 59–60, 192–193, 203
Heartbreak, curing, 59–60, 188, 192–193, 194, 195–196, 208–209
Home blessing, 137–139, 140–141
Horses, 41–42, 49–50. *See also* Pets
In-laws, getting along with, 142–143
Jealousy, ending, 28, 29
Kissing, 121–122. *See also* Passion

INDEX

Love letters, 104, 114–115
Love
  attracting, 54, 56, 57, 58,
    61–62, 62–63, 64–65,
    134
  compelling someone to,
    68–69
  ending
    for a friend, 27
    from a friend, 26
    for past lovers, 197
  finding, 69, 71–80
    in autumn, 76–78
    in spring, 73
    in summer, 74–76
    in winter, 78–80
  most, from suitor, 88
  gone wrong, 144, 191
  in your home, 135, 136–139
  lasting, 132, 133, 134,
    176–177, 180–181
  letting go of, 190, 191
  spreading to friends, 23–24
  true, 61
  unrequited, 58, 194
  welcoming, 54
Marriage, 166–183
  ensuring, 166
  knowing if you should, 166
  proposals
    getting, 167–168
    yes answer, 168.

  See also Relationships,
    Weddings
Marriage, 96, 98–99, 100
Memories, passionate
  forgetting, 186
  remembering, 116–117
Negative energy, reversing,
  60–61, 151, 206–207
Parties, good energy for, 20–22
Passion
  increasing, 112, 113, 114,
    118, 119, 120, 123, 124
  ending, 199–200
  reawakening, 121, 125
  wedding night, 181–182
Pets, 39–51
  adopting, 47
  attracting, 41, 46–47
  communicating with, 50–51
  love for humans, 40, 41, 42,
    43–45
  other pets, love amongst,
    39, 41
  significant other, love for,
    40–41
  transforming into human, 51
Promposal, 85
Proposals. *See* Marriage,
  proposals
Protection, 139–140, 156–157,
  157–158, 161, 163
Purity, 71–73

Queen of Cups, 100–102
Reconciling, 153, 154–155
Relationships
   commitment in, 89, 132
   fights in, 150–151, 152
   future of 94–95
   good luck in, 141
   long distance, 133
   peaceful, 147–150, 150–151
   saving, 146–147
   truth in, 145
   See also Breaking up; Love, lasting; Unfaithfulness
Romance. See Passion
Roommates, 33–34
Safekeeping. See Protection
Self confidence, increasing, 55–56
Sex
   enhancing, 129
   hiding flaws during, 126–127
   new ideas during stopping, 128
   trying, 125–126
   See also Passion
Snakes, 48. See also Pets
Spouses. See Marriage, Relationships

Spring, finding love in, 73
Stalkers, getting rid of, 202–203
Summer, finding love in, 74–76
Tea, love, 64–65
Texts
   incantations before, 115–116
   stopping, 199
Truth telling, 145, 146
Unbinding spell, 196–197
Unfaithfulness, 108
   preventing, 133, 146–147
   stopping, 145
Vows, writing, 169–170
Weddings, 169–183
   after-wedding ritual, 182–183
   before-wedding ritual, 170–171
   good luck for, 172–173, 173–174, 176, 180
   free of conflict, 175, 178–179
   jitters, curing, 172
   vows, writing, 169–170
   weather, good, 176
Winter, finding love in, 78–80